D1599025

Legacy of Thasos

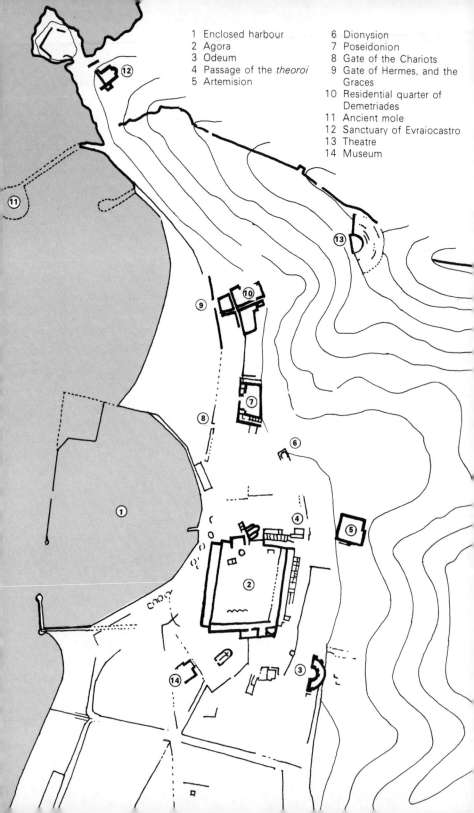

1 Enclosed harbour
2 Agora
3 Odeum
4 Passage of the *theoroi*
5 Artemision
6 Dionysion
7 Poseidonion
8 Gate of the Chariots
9 Gate of Hermes, and the Graces
10 Residential quarter of Demetriades
11 Ancient mole
12 Sanctuary of Evraiocastro
13 Theatre
14 Museum

Legacy of
Thasos

R. J. L. Wynne-Thomas

Springwood Books

ISBN 0 9059 4765 7

Printed in Great Britain by
Butler & Tanner Ltd,
Frome and London

Contents

Contents

Illustrations

Illustrations

Foreword

I have never visited Thasos, I am ashamed to say, and I am thus the least qualified person to write a Foreword for this book. The few lines which follow are meant as a kind of introduction to Joan Wynne-Thomas by someone who has known her for many years.

There is no doubt that islands are a source of infinite fascination for those people who have an eye for beauty, and who wish to conceive of life in all its aspects, from antiquity to the present day.

Joan Wynne-Thomas fell in love with Cyprus in 1969, and since then has remained faithful to the island in spite of all the misfortunes which have struck both the country and its people in the years which followed. Her enthusiasm for archaeology took her to all the archaeological sites, but she particularly favoured the shores of Salamis and the Karpass, where she chose to live.

Although she cannot claim to have become an expert 'digger' she tasted the hardships, and the delights of field work at Kition, where she was very much liked and appreciated by all members of the staff, archaeologists and labourers alike.

Though the adverse political conditions have kept her away from the island since 1974, her interest and sympathy for Cyprus and the island have not diminished, and this she has demonstrated both with her pen, and with her generosity.

Many Cypriots remember her as the organizer of a Bradfield College Greek play (Sophocles' Philoktetes) in the ancient theatre at Salamis – a memorable performance.

Her new love – Thasos – will no doubt give her as many satisfactions as Cyprus did. The monuments, the people, the climate, may differ from those of Cyprus; but there is an element which unites them both; their Greek past, and present.

Joan Wynne-Thomas moves as comfortably in Thasos as she did in Cyprus, and her guidance to the beauties and antiquities of this island will be intelligent and enchanting for all those who will chose her as a guide.

VASSOS KARAGEORGHIS
Director of Antiquities for Cyprus

Preface

Before my first visit to Thasos I searched long and diligently for a comprehensive study in English about this island, which had – particularly in the earlier stages of its occupation – played so important a part in the life and trade of the north Aegean sea; which had such interesting and well-excavated ruins; and which, above all, is so very beautiful, and in contrast to most Greek islands, so very green. Nothing appeared to be forthcoming, and this book is the result of two seasons' work in the island, and very considerable research in this country.

Although it is, obviously, not a work for scholars – something I am not qualified to write – it is hoped that it will be of interest and assistance to the English-speaking educated and intelligent visitors who visit the island in increasing numbers every year, and even to some people in this country who long, as I do, to be in Greece!

My grateful thanks are due to the French School in Athens for their permission to reproduce their maps of the island; for their courtesy in allowing me to use the photograph (p. 114) of the impresssed seal of a wine-amphora; and for their encouraging good wishes. I also had the good fortune to know two of their former excavators in Thasos – Professor Jean Pouilloux, and Professor Georges Roux – while I was working with Dr Karageorghis in Cyprus.

My thanks are particularly due to John Hopkins, the tireless Librarian of the Society of Antiquaries of London, for his searchings for Journals and records in the library of that Society, invariably on the highest shelves, reached only by spiral iron staircases; to Dr Frank Stubbings, of Emmanuel College, Cambridge, for his help and encouragement; and to Richard Youdale, Classics Master at Bradfield College, for his help with translations.

To my publishers, particularly in the person of Christopher Foster, I would like to express my appreciation of their enthusiasm, interest and courtesy, as well as much help.

Finally, to the writer of the Foreword to this book, with whom I was privileged to work in Cyprus, and whose help, patience and instruction then have gone far towards enabling me to attempt this study: to Dr Vassos Karageorghis I would say

$$\mu\varepsilon \; \pi o\lambda\lambda\acute{\varepsilon}\varsigma \; \kappa\iota' \; \grave{\varepsilon}\gamma\kappa\acute{\alpha}\rho\delta\iota\varepsilon\varsigma \; \varepsilon\grave{\vartheta}\chi\alpha\rho\iota\sigma\tau\acute{\iota}\varepsilon\varsigma$$

JOAN L. WYNNE-THOMAS
Thasos-Bucklebury
1975–1977

1

Introduction to Thasos

Thasos is the most northerly island of the Aegean sea – 25 kilometres from north to south, and 21 kilometres from east to west at its farthest points. Unlike other islands in the Aegean it is thickly wooded, mainly with conifers and olives, and has a fairly high rainfall. It is mountainous; and the highest peak, Mount Hypsarion, rises to 1203 metres. The soil is mainly a grey-green gneiss, veined with mica, and a beautiful white marble with large, rather coarse crystals, which attracted many sculptors and artists during the periods of the island's greatness, and particularly during the fourth century BC.

This century saw the full flowering of Classical art, with the history of Greece influencing the evolution of architectural structures; and also a considerable widening in scope and vision of the very great sculptors who lived at this time such as Praxitiles and Scopas, both of whom had schools in Thasos, and whose work was commissioned by Thasian citizens.

Fine temples had been erected in many places in Greece including the island during the Archaic period, but the fourth century – following the Persian wars, and the later dominance of Athens – saw a cohesion in design and in planned 'city-state' building hitherto unknown. This was particularly so in the eastern Greek cities, which had suffered considerably, but whose philosophical, political and moral life and traditions had, none the less, survived.

Dominated, as building programmes were, by local stone, Thasos was indeed fortunate to possess so much marble, and the fourth century city must truly have presented a superb sight to the traveller approaching by the only route – then as now – in a boat, across the sea.

Throughout the island there is little top-soil, and every foot of it is made use of by the modern Thasian citizen. They are farmers, fruit-growers, growers of olives, and keepers of bees – in hundreds of thousands. They are workers in timber, quarriers of marble, and tenders of vines. They are fishermen, fishing mainly at night with flares, and usually with three small boats towed by a larger one. Some of the young men go abroad to earn more money, but having made it return always to the island to build better houses for their families. The religion of the island is ninety-eight per cent Orthodox Greek.

The island has two small towns – the capital Thasos, sometimes called Limin – which is at the eastern end of the north coast with fine natural harbours sheltered by the Point of Evraiocastro; and Liminaria in the south-west, which is little more than a fishing village.

There are half-a-dozen hill villages, and a few small settlements round the coast; and altogether there is a population of rather under 18,000 inhabitants.

One main road, with its two exits from the town of Thasos less than 100 yards apart, runs completely round the island and connects with lesser roads leading to the hill villages; yet here was the capital city of the sixth century BC northern Aegean, and of eastern Macedonia, and here today is one of the most interesting and rewarding archaeological sites in the whole of Greece. To quote Peter Levi, well-known in the world of classical scholarship – 'the surviving antiquities of Thasos are some of the most wonderful in Greece'.

The first archaeological excavation took place in 1863, and although undoubtedly profitable was unhappily 'hasty and destructive'. Some early work was also done on the translation of the texts.

During the first decade of the twentieth century J. ff. Baker-Penoyre spent five months in the island, and made some interesting discoveries. However, systematic excavation did not really start until 1911 when the French School in Athens began work, at this time represented by Charles Picard, Adolphe Reinach, and Charles Avezou. Unhappily both Reinach and Avezou were killed in the 1914–1918 war, and little headway was made until a team led by Marcel Launey started excavating during the 1930s.

Work was again interrupted by the 1939–1945 war, but was re-started in 1954 by a team under M. Jean Pouilloux, also from the French School, and since that date excavation has continued during every season. There has also been annual archaeological publication in the *Bulletin de Correspondance Hellénique*. (BCH)

The island is reputed to have had an original Phoenician settlement dating from 1500 BC, and Herodotus has a certain amount to say about this; but the main colonization did not take place until the seventh century BC, when, in response to an Oracle from Delphi, an expedition sailed from Paros under the leadership of Telesikles – the father or grandfather of the poet Archilochos. In a short hundred years from this date Thasos had become the capital city of the area, with many colonies on the mainland, great wealth from gold-mines and other sources, and a very considerable trade with both the east and the west.

The main archaeological site with its agora, cult-buildings, odeum, great main street, and so forth, is in the centre of the little modern town which, in turn, is entirely enclosed within the walls of the ancient city; and many of the gates, with their fine bas-relief carvings, stand in gardens of flowers owned by modern Thasian inhabitants.

The Acropolis is some 140 metres above the town with truly mag-nificent views in every direction, and the sea on three sides. Here are the foundations of a temple to the Pythian Apollo; the fine remains of a temple to Athena Poliouchos – protectress of the city – and a little simple sanctuary, dedicated to Pan, which has enthralled both scholars and visitors for many years.

The sanctuary of the god Dionysos, whose cult swept Greece dur-ing the seventh and sixth centuries BC, and the theatre – which was, of course connected with this cult – are both within the walls of the ancient city, as are the cult-buildings of other gods, as well as those heroes who were also worshipped in the island.

Many of the beautiful objects which have been excavated over the years are in the local museum, which stands in a garden of roses, but there are also Thasian finds in the Louvre; in Istanbul; and in other places. Oddly there is not much in Athens.

In the Thasos museum the most noteworthy piece is a marble head of Dionysos which is attributed to Praxitiles. This shows the god in the Hellenistic style as an inspiration for artists and intellectuals, and in particular for the Greek tragic poets. The statue, of which this is the head, was at one time the centrepiece of the exedra of the Dionysion.

There is much else of interest in the museum including an Archaic bronze of the goddess Artemis, and some good examples of pottery from the early Thasian school whose workshop was found in the Artemision.

Marble head of Dionysos— 3rd century B C School of Praxitiles. Found in the Dionysion before 1959

An interesting feature of the excavations has always been the discovery of so many and varied texts in a number of different places on the site, and particularly in the strange underground building known as the Passage of the *theoroi*, those eponymous magistrates of which the island possessed so many. These texts, which include lists of officials, the constitution of various councils, the dates of many festivals, lists of priests of the cults, and records of ancient names, together with the writings of Herodotus – who visited the island – make it possible to reconstruct the life of the Thasian people during the Archaic, Classical, and Hellenistic periods in considerable detail; and some of these texts are as late as the period of Roman domination.

There are also the writings of Hippocrates who lived in the island for more than three years to help verify details of places, and also of people, which would otherwise have been lost to posterity in the mists of time. He also wrote at some length about the climate of the island.

Thasos had its own coinage of which there are some interesting examples extant – including one or two in gold – and as has already been mentioned much pottery has been found. In addition to that which was locally made, examples from other districts including Corinth, Ionia, Rhodes, and the Cyclades have been excavated, which underlines the far-reaching trade which the island enjoyed.

Marble is everywhere and is still quarried and exported from the Aliki area in the south-east of the island. There is also an interesting small sanctuary at Aliki, and the remains of an early Christian church.

The Thasian gold-mines are said to have been situated between Aliki and Kinyra, and slightly to the north of the island of that name, however, the actual site has still to be discovered. The island also owned gold-mines on the mainland near Mount Pangeum, and at Scapte Hyle, which were the real source of her very considerable wealth.

Thasian wine was famous and was another major export, and the wine-jars – with their impressed seals – have been found all round the eastern Mediterranean and as far afield as Egypt and Sicily.

Despite setbacks and wars Thasos managed to maintain a certain independence and individuality, as indeed she does today. Her periods of true greatness were during the seventh century BC, and again, after a time of considerable tribulation, during the fourth century BC when the great re-building programme took place, of which each year more and more is being brought to light, by the techniques of modern archaeological skill.

Some Oriental influence is apparent in such things as the *phylakoi* (the guardian gods) at the gates of the city, and in some of the discoveries made in the Heraklion, and elsewhere. This is again a testimony to Thasian individuality in a Greek world.

The islanders also tended to deify their heroes, and both Theogenes – the Olympic boxer, who was born Thasian – and the general Glaukos – a friend of Archilochos, and one of the original colonizers – had cult-buildings and statues in the agora.

Every hero has many legends connected with his name; the gods have much that is historical in their background, and in this island, as in so much of Greece, myth and legend are interwoven with historical fact and proven archaeological discovery.

Background from 700 BC until Byzantium

Herodotus gives us two definite accounts of early Phoenician settlements in the island of Thasos. The first, in Book 2 is obviously a straight statement of fact, although there are some scholars who argue against any Phoenician settlement at all. It is surely unlikely that this was an inaccuracy, particularly as Herodotus lived some 2000 years nearer in time to the period in question. It is, however, true that the French excavators, who have done the great part of the archaeological work so far accomplished in the island, have discovered few traces of any settlement earlier than the first Parian colonization which took place during the early part of the seventh century BC.

Herodotus states '... and I have also been to Thasos, where I found a temple of Herakles built by the Phoenicians who settled there after they had sailed in search of Europa ...'

Referring as this does to the Phoenician expedition to try to find

The Aegean Sea in the Archaic period

Europa after she had been carried off by the Zeus bull, it would also account for the persistent tradition that the heroic Kadmos is in some way connected with the island; and that his son – or nephew – Thasos was, indeed, the first settler, and gave the island his name.

To refer again to Herodotus, in Book 6, 'Much the most remarkable (mines) are those discovered by the Phoenicians who came with Thasos, the son of Phoenix, to colonize the island which has since borne his name ...'

The possible discovery of gold in the island would have been a valid reason for a Phoenician landing. A Semitic people from the south they had settled in a coastal strip on the eastern side of the 'Inner sea', and their peripatetic trading was largely conditioned by the confines of their country. This was a narrow strip of land, bounded on one side by the sea, and backed by high mountain ranges. First and foremost they were traders, and an island so well-placed as Thasos in the north Aegean could not but attract them. No pottery has, as yet, been discovered with earlier decoration than Sub-Geometric, but there are one or two Semitic proper names in the island to this day.

As far as archaeological excavation is concerned, during the 1961 season some traces of inhabitation were found which corresponded to a period slightly earlier than the installation of the oldest columns of the ancient city, but little else before the Parian colonization has, so far, come to light.

Some consideration of the geographical position of Thasos should be taken into account to show how vitally important an island in this position could have been to east–west relations; to naval strategy; and above all to the value of its position on the sea-lane trade routes.

The main occupation of the island, which has continued to be occupied from then to the present day, took place during the early part of the seventh century BC, and the generally acknowledged date is 680 BC. This is endorsed by the French School in Athens, but Dr N. G. L. Hammond – to quote one Greek historian – puts it as early as 710 BC.

The response of the Pythian Apollo to a request from Paros is possibly the only authentic Oracle to have been preserved. In the usual hexametres is announced 'Telesikles – I bid you announce to the people of Paros "Found now a city far-seen. In the Isle of Mists. I command so."' Or in another, and rather lesser translation 'Announce to the Parians, O Telesikles, that I bid you found a conspicuous city on the island of Eëria'.

Colonization by the Greeks followed an almost ritual pattern. The settlement 'far from home' was created by a party of colonists with a leader. Sacred fire from the hearth of their city was taken with them for the ceremonial founding of the new *polis* or 'city state', and inevitably the original customs, cults, and political institutions of the new colony were those of the place from which the colonizers had come.

Thasos from this time maintained a certain individuality which has continued, and does so still.

Without question, some earlier, and more eastern civilization exerted an influence on the island at some time, as is seen, in the erection of *phylakoi* (guardian gods) at the gates of the city, a custom which is more Oriental than Greek; and there is also certain evidence, not wholly undisputed, in the excavated temple of Herakles, which bears witness to an earlier Asiatic god of the same name – doubtless Herodotus' Herakles of the Phoenicians.

M. Jean Pouilloux, who, as leader of the French concession was responsible for some years for excavation in the island, writes of Greek and native culture in contact, which presumes some tribe already living in the island at the time of Telesikles' arrival. Without doubt the island has always had a mixed population, and although it has been called a 'rampart of Hellenism' many inscriptions bear names of Thracian origin.

It is known that the people of Paros owned at least one penteconter (50-oared boat) which was built for them during the seventh century BC, but there are no indications that the colonization of Thasos was anything but peaceful. However, a reinforcement party of settlers, which included mercenaries, followed the original expedition, mainly to provide protection from raiding parties from the mainland. This contingent was led by the poet Archilochos, who was either a son, or a grandson of Telesikles. The island was rich in natural resources, and doubtless attracted many adventurers as well as serious merchants in search of new openings for their trade, and some mercenaries were necessary for protection.

The foundation of *polis* became one of the main sources of strength and stability of Greece, and the founders usually had good relationships with their colonies.

With the opening of the entrance of the Euxine sea, beyond the sea of Propontis, a very considerable new trade route was created along the coasts of Thrace and Macedonia, with Thasos in a key position on this route. In the stormy conditions of the north Aegean the island's sheltered natural harbours must have provided a much needed haven for many ships caught in violent storms; and considerable trade would have come about naturally in this way.

In a short century from Telesikles' landing the town of Thasos became the first city of the area, with many colonies of its own on the mainland. These were Neapolis (the modern Kavala) Galepsos, Datum, Oesyme, and Krenides – better known later as Philippi. During the later part of the sixth century Thasos also owned Scapte Hyle, of which Herodotus writes: 'The island's revenue was derived partly from property on the mainland, and partly from mines: the gold mines at Scapte Hyle alone yielded in all eighty talents a year ... '

At this time relations between the island and mainland Greece were satisfactory, and the Oracle of the Pythian Apollo was consulted on many major issues.

The island also had a considerable trade with Macedonia, and in particular with the Chalkidike. Thasos produced gold, timber for ship-building, and large quantities of wine, while the Chalkidike grew olives, vines and cereals. The mainland colonies produced gold, silver, and wheat, and there were also silver mines on the island.

For a time, at any rate, the island continued to prosper until, during the early part of the fifth century BC, they became involved in the wars with Persia. Darius having taken over command of the Persian army – in the words of Herodotus 'superseded all his other generals' – and having assembled a considerable fleet, crossed the Hellespont, and accompanied by an army of formidable proportions proceeded to march through northern Greece. Fate, however, had much in store which Darius had not expected, and if for no other reason than his vivid descriptive language Herodotus shall again take up the tale.

From Thasos the fleet stood across to the mainland and proceeded along the coast to Acanthus, and from there attempted to double Athos; but before they were round this promontary they were caught by a violent northerly gale which proved too much for the ships to cope with. A great many of them were driven ashore and wrecked on Athos – indeed report says that something like 300 were lost, with over 20,000 men. The sea in the neighbourhood is full of monsters so that those of the ship's companies who were not dashed to pieces on the rocks were seized and devoured. Others, unable to swim, were drowned; others died of cold.

The following year Darius ordered the Thasians to dismantle their defences, and sail their fleet to the mainland port of Abdera – which they did. However, their considerable resources made them determined to strengthen their defences, and build themselves a number of warships. Later, when the Persian army, which by then was commanded by Xerxes, was billeted on their mainland colonies, a Thasian named Antipaster, son of Orgeus, a 'citizen of the highest repute' had to provide a meal for them which cost him 400 talents of silver.

After the assassination of Xerxes in 465 BC the dangers attendant on the advances made by the Persians receded, and the democratic leaders of Athens came into power. In this changed situation relations between Athens and Sparta were finally severed. Athens was now the leader of the Athenian Alliance and was in a position of considerable strength, and among preparations for another war she enlarged her fleet every year. In 465 BC Thasos seceded from the Athenian Alliance in protest against claims from them that they should be allowed to share in the gold-mining, and other prosperous enterprises which the island enjoyed by reason of her considerable mainland possessions.

The commercial prosperity of Thasos was, however, far too strong a temptation for the Athenians, and their fleet – commanded by Cimon – attacked and defeated the Thasians, capturing thirty of their men-of-war. Troops were landed, and at the same time a number of settlers were brought by the Athenians to the districts round Scapte

Hyle, and also to the Strymon valley – the main area of Thasian colonial gold. Thasos now appealed in secret to Sparta for help. In their appeal they pointed out that if Sparta would invade Attica some of the pressure would be withdrawn from the island, and Athenian interest would be concentrated elsewhere. No treaty had been signed between Sparta and Thasos, but the Spartans were overwhelmingly aware of the ambition of their great rival, and not unnaturally in some fear of what she might do. Any action which they might have taken was, however, interfered with by a shattering earthquake in 464 BC, which killed more than 20,000 people in the city of Sparta alone.

In 463 BC Thasos capitulated, becoming a city of secondary importance, and according to Thucydides '... they pulled down their ramparts, and handed over their fleet, at the same time giving up their continental possessions, and mines ...' Following this very unhappy state of affairs they apparently even had difficulty in finding their tribute money. For at least ten years the prosperity of the island, and its recovery, were threatened, although from records the annual tribute paid was increased from three to thirty talents by 446 BC, which was perhaps a sign that Thasos was again beginning to raise her head.

During the unhappy period of occupation, and the despair which must have accompanied it, there was much unrest among the Thasians. Evidence of this is shown on an inscribed marble tablet which was found by the excavators in the agora. This reads: 'A reward of 1000 staters will be paid by the city to anyone who denounces a rebellion against Thasos, and whose words turn out to be true. If the informer is a slave he will be given his freedom. If there is more than one informer three citizens will act as judges in a court of justice. If the informer is himself a member of the plot he will get the reward.' This is evidence enough that the occupiers were far from being in full control. The date of this order was 21 Apatourion, and it was signed under the archonship of Acryptos, Aleximachos, and Dexiades. The archons were the chief magistrates of the city, and these three were either officers of the invading forces, or elected by them.

In 425 BC there were more than 300 states paying tribute to Athens, and the more these states prospered the higher the tribute money would be. In 390 BC Thrasybulus was conducting a major naval campaign for Athens in the Aegean, and was virtually unopposed. He was more peaceable in his outlook than many of his predecessors, and obtained a satisfactory alliance with Thasos, among other places.

Gradually the Athenian Alliance grew into an Athenian Empire to which it became of importance that conquered districts and vassal states such as Naxos, Aegina and Thasos, should recover some of their individuality, and therefore prosperity.

In the period of peace which followed much benefit was derived from being a part of the Athenian Empire, and in addition protection was forthcoming, not only from piratical raiding parties, but also from Persia.

Currency regulations were relaxed, and Thasos was permitted to coin in silver; and in time some of her mainland possessions were restored to her.

During the fourth century BC a very considerable programme of re-building and re-organization took place, and the city which is coming to light as the result of modern excavation is, with certain exceptions, the city of Thasos which was built and restored at this time.

The 'Thasian continent' was re-organized, and to some extent re-established, and in 360 BC the Orator, Kallistratos, founded Krenides with Thasian help. This colony, which was close to Mount Pangeum, was rich because of its gold. A short time later Krenides was visited by King Philip of Macedonia, who not only took over the gold-mines, but changed the name of the city from Krenides to Philippi, by which name it was known at the time of St Paul, and is still so called to this day.

Gradually the 'polis' of Thasos began to recover, and new ramparts were built consisting of a very considerable wall, with gates and towers. This encircled the whole city excepting on the north side, which was protected by the sea. The harbours were again full of ships, and the ship-building yards towards the Point of Evraiocastro once more worked to capacity. These shipyards are still in use, although the ships built there today are mainly large caiques, and other fishing boats.

Ruins of the Thasian colony of Krenides (Philippi)

Close to the port the foundations of the agora were laid, and buildings were constructed in accordance with the new requirements of the Thasian citizens, many near the sanctuary of Zeus Agoraios, who was regarded as the great civilizing influence of the time.

The Archives of the city were brought up to date, and lists of the principal magistrates and functionaries, both religious and secular, were engraved on the walls of many of the public buildings. These, with other inscriptions found by the excavators, have enabled a very complete list of institutions of the fourth century BC, and of the Hellenistic period, to be recorded. The once-again economic strength of the Thasians also gave them a certain political independence, and they were able to regain something of the individuality which had always been one of their most outstanding characteristics, and which has characterized the people of the island to the present day.

By 343 BC appreciation of the protection afforded by Athens was such that Thasos assented to a request for a base on the island for Athenian mercenary troops.

The Pax Romana brought even more prosperity to the city, and some interesting Roman remains have been excavated, although certain buildings, and in particular the theatre, suffered during this period.

Unfortunately the history of the following epoch – that of Byzantium – has been almost entirely lost.

From the flood of light which has been let in on past centuries, and the confirmation of that which is often, here as elsewhere, historical surmise, the excavations in Thasos have been very rewarding; and in addition to the re-construction of so many buildings, many records – as well as objects – have been recovered. These help to paint for posterity a vivid picture of the island and its life during the Archaic, Classical and Hellenistic periods.

Much change had taken place during these centuries, and many famous people had lived.

COMPARATIVE TABLE   *All dates approximate*

BC	THASOS	GREECE	W. MEDITERRANEAN	FAMOUS MEN
1500	*Assumed landing of Phoenicians*	*Mycenaean, and late Minoan culture. Early shaft graves*		
680 to	*Colonization by Paros* / *Archilochos' first poetry preserved*	*Doric wooden temple of Hera at Olympia*	*Paestum Syracuse Selinus*	*Archilochos dies (664.)*
582		*First Pythian games at Delphi* / *Ionian School of Philosophy*		
500		*Persian War and invasion of Greece*		*Herodotus born at Halicarnassos in 484* / *Theogenes wins Olympic boxing*
480		*Xerxes' Invasion*	*Victory coins at Syracuse*	*Hippocrates born on Cos, in 460*
465	*Thasos secedes and capitulates*	*Temple of Zeus built at Olympia*	*Democracy at Syracuse*	*Polygnotos of Thasos dies (443)*
449		*Peace signed with Persia*	*Herodotus settles in Thuria in Italy. Dies (425)*	
409	*Euripides at Pella in Macedonia. Writes Bacchae in 407. Dies (406)*			
390-on	*Great re-building programme of city*	*End of city states*	*King of Southern Italy is the Spartan Archidamos III*	*Praxitiles Scopas*

2

The enclosed archaeological site. Walls, gates, towers.
Agora, Odeum, Main street (or Sacred Way). Cult-
buildings within the agora. Residential quarter of
Demetriades

During the year 1909 John Baker-Penoyre published the results of
his work during a five months' stay in Thasos in the *Journal of the
Society for the Promotion of Hellenic Studies*; of which learned society
he was, at that time, both Secretary and Librarian.

During this visit he had made a thorough survey of the walls, with
scale plans and drawings. These walls, which must have been originally of the Archaic period, were part of the great fourth century BC
programme of rebuilding, and had then been much strengthened and
fortified; as had the many towers which were used by the guard for
look-out and other military purposes.

Unfortunately Baker-Penoyre started his survey at the north-east
corner near the Point of Evraiocastro, and he therefore missed the
three gates between this point and the agora. Much of the wall
between these gates and the north-eastern corner had been destroyed
by monks from the monastery of Vatopedi on Mount Athos in their
re-building of a *metochi* (farm) which they owned in this area during
the early part of the twentieth century. This was surrounded by a
vineyard – now an olive grove – and it was from the eastern side of
this vineyard that surveys and measurements began. With the recent
excavation of the agora, and its nearby residential area known as the
Field of Demetriades, the three gates in this stretch have now been
cleared.

The first, or most westerly of these is mostly destroyed and has no
bas-relief carving; however the next two are in excellent condition

and are both decorated. From the direction of the agora is first the well-preserved gate of the Goddess of the Chariots, a massive construction of marble opening to the north-west, and standing in the garden of a modern Thasian citizen. The foundations of this gate are of heavy blocks of marble, and the quadrangular uprights are entire – only the lintel is missing. The system used for opening and closing this gate is also particularly well preserved. The bas-relief carving, which is beautifully executed, and preserved excepting for the faces, shows a chariot drawn by two horses. In the chariot stands a young goddess, in *chiton* and *himation* vertically pleated. The god Hermes, here shown with a beard, leads the horses, and it has been suggested that the goddess is Artemis.

A short distance further east, and opposite the entrance to the Demetriades residential area, is the Gate of Hermes and the Graces, which has been sometimes erroneously referred to as the Gate of Semele. The reliefs on the right-hand column are more worn than that on the previous gate, but are none the less easily decipherable. As always the hands and upper parts of the bodies are most worn, and the faces are almost gone. Hermes is naked, excepting for a cloak which hangs from his shoulders. He is walking towards the centre of the city, with his three companion Graces following closely behind.

Gate of Hermes and the Graces

The Gate of the Chariots

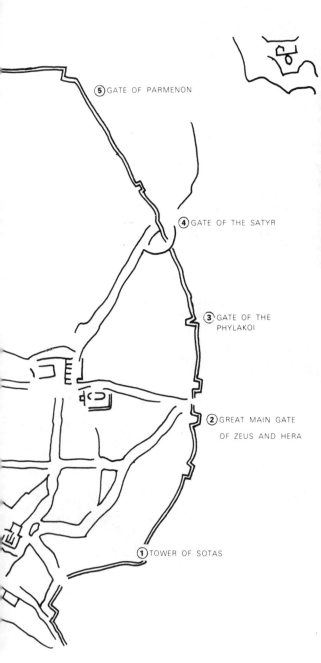

⑤ GATE OF PARMENON

④ GATE OF THE SATYR

③ GATE OF THE
PHYLAKOI

② GREAT MAIN GATE
OF ZEUS AND HERA

① TOWER OF SOTAS

Part of the Eastern Wall

*The gates of the
Western Wall*

To the east of this gate is a flight of steps, built of gneiss, which takes the perimeter road on to a higher level at this point within the walls. From the north-eastern corner, at the Point of Evraiocastro, the ancient city wall again appears, at this point in a good state of preservation, and very well excavated and restored.

At the start there are three courses of (ashlar) masonry which, according to the Baker-Penoyre survey, measure approx: 1 metre by 40 centimetres. After the right-angle turn on to the path which leads to the theatre, and then to the Acropolis, there is a short stretch of rather unequal building; however this is followed by a long, continuous reach which contains polygonal blocks of considerable size, well-adjusted and practically upright. Despite brambles, rubble and much soil this was noted in the 1907 survey.

At the end of this stretch stands the remains of a tower, which has not been restored.

This town wall is a fine example of building work of the late fifth, or early fourth centuries BC. The locally quarried marble, laid in vast blocks which are occasionally interspersed with blocks of the island's mica-veined grey-green gneiss, is of course responsible for much of the beauty of the city of Thasos, and this is certainly so with the city wall.

Beyond the entrance to the theatre is a stretch which reaches to the Acropolis where there are first the remains of a temple dedicated to Apollo. This was destroyed by Christians during the thirteenth century AD, in order to build a vast mediaeval citadel; the foundations of both temple, and later citadel, being in many places only a strengthening of the natural rock, mainly because the land to the south-east falls sharply away.

There is a small section of wall to the north-east of the temple of Athena, but substantial remains do not occur again until the highest level is reached, which is beyond the Sanctuary of Pan. At this point the hill is some 150 metres above the sea.

From this level there is a sharply-inclined downward stretch, which ends in a right-angle turn and the Gate of Parmenon, which was signed by the worker in marble 'Parmenon made me' somewhere between 510 and 490 BC. This gate was described by Baker-Penoyre as a signed masterpiece of engineering skill, and the stretch of wall below it as the best that he had found. Within the right-angle turn there is a staircase which it is still possible to descend.

There are four towers in this stretch, and one more gate before the south – carved – gate of Silenos. Here again the wall is well built, with massive aligned blocks, and it must have afforded considerable protection from the rest of the island, and from any raiding parties which might land in the south.

The gate is set at an oblique angle in the ramparts, and is strongly fortified. On the left-hand pillar, which is quadrangular, an immense satyr is carved, holding a *kantharos*. The figure is ithyphallic, and wears the soft boots of the tragic actor. To the front of the figure, just within the gate, is a small niche for votive offerings. This is the oldest carved gate of the fortifications, and dates from the end of the sixth century BC.

The next stretch of wall, leading nearly to the gate of the Guardian Gods of the city (*phylakoi*) is still in process of excavation, and has the same pattern of fine building; with huge, well-balanced blocks of marble, and excellent construction. This tragic gate of the *phylakoi* is now being excavated, and a large amount of it has been beautifully restored, but nothing can replace the bas-relief carvings which should be there. These carvings showed the two guardian gods – the demi-gods of Mount Olympos, Dionysos and Herakles – and the bas-reliefs dated from approximately 506 BC.

As far as is known there was a large carved block on one side, show-ing Dionysos and his *thiasos*, while on the other stood the figures of both *phylakoi*. All the reliefs were roughly torn from their backgrounds by early excavators, and taken to Istanbul. Dionysos was lost in transit, but the figure of Herakles, here shown as an archer, is still in the museum there. This figure of Herakles appeared at one time on the Thasian coinage, and examples of this are in the local museum.

To the left of these two figures was the usual small niche for offer-ings from travellers passing through the gate.

The relief of Dionysos and his procession of satyrs and maenads

Ithyphallic Silenos at gate of that n

Steps and wall by the phylakoi gate, recently excavated

which was taken from the opposite wall is only known from a clumsy drawing made by a Thasian doctor called Christides.

An inscription was found on the gate which read 'Zeus, Semele, and Alkmene set up their children as guardians of the city'. *IG. XII. 8.*

To the south of this gate a fine staircase has recently been uncovered which leads to the top of the walls; but the next stretch of the fortifications, which contains two towers, has yet to be excavated. However the ramparts of this section are easily discernible.

The great main gate of the city is now reached, and today this is almost surrounded by olive trees which serve to enhance its beauty. It is the Gate of Zeus and Hera, which together with the gate of the

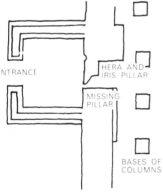

The Gate of Zeus and Hera – the main gate into the city.
The relief on the pillar is of the goddess Hera, and Iris,
her messenger

phylakoi guarded the city from the south-western plain, and from the sea towards the mainland of Greece.

This gate had stood from shortly after the Parian colonization, but was rebuilt during the fourth century BC programme of rebuilding, and strengthening of fortifications.

A sturdy bastion had its walls crowned in the Doric style, which helped to increase the city's protection from the modern weapons and methods of war. Within this bastion was a monumental inner façade, which was decorated, and there were two rows of pillars. Those at ground level being quadrangular Doric columns; those of the upper layer consisting of square pilasters, with quadrangular Ionic half-columns attached. As will be realized this was a considerable change from the accepted style of Greek architecture of the Classical period.

Two square marble pillars flanked the gate, decorated with bas-reliefs of the principal god of Mount Olympos – Zeus – and his wife Hera, and the royal couple were shown giving orders to their personal messengers, Hermes and Iris.

The south pillar, which showed Zeus with the 'silver-tongued Hermes' is unhappily now destroyed, although some fragments of it are in the museum, but the opposite pillar, a vast square block of Thasian marble, still stands. On this is depicted the goddess Hera, clad in a pleated *chiton*, seated on a throne, and giving her orders to Iris. The goddess is facing away from the city, and except for a little weathering this relief is in good condition.

Beyond this gate to the north-west and towards the sea excavation still continues, with two more towers, and the last gate still to be uncovered.

Although it is now nearly seventy years since John Baker-Penoyre made his careful and painstaking survey, which can only have been accomplished with considerable difficulty, and without the reward of finding any gate but that of Parmenon, modern excavators owe him much thanks, which fact was acknowledged by Charles Picard. who, gratefully, recorded the help derived by the French School from the plans and maps which were the result of Baker-Penoyre's early work.

Part of the five acre site of the agora

Doric columns of the north-west portico of the agora
Base of statues, or altar, in the north-west portico of the main site of the agora

At the eastern side of the city, within the walls and not far from the harbours, is an area of some four to five acres which was the site of the agora, the centre of the civic and commercial life of Thasos which also contained some of the cult-buildings, and statues and tombs of heroes and famous men.

Considerable excavation has taken place here since 1948, and the whole plan – with the remains of many buildings, is now reasonably clear.

There are four great porticos, those ambulatory edifices which played so large a part in the life of ancient Greek cities. That to the north-west is the best preserved, and was built at some time during the re-building period of the fourth century BC. It is over 97 metres long, and built entirely of marble. The portico was closed on three sides with walls, but was open to the agora through a colonnade of 35 Doric pillars *in antis*. Unusually there was no central colonnade to support the whole.

Standing within the agora it is not difficult to picture the life of the city. To the north-west stood this great colonnade, peopled with an ever-moving throng of Greek citizens about the daily life and business of this thriving capital; with the philosophers and teachers in their favourite places, standing on a step, or seated on a marble bench, declaiming to those Thasians who sat at their feet; and soldiers of the guard, off-duty, moving among the citizens. To the north-east and south-east two more porticos, also built of marble; and to the north the winged edifice 'Paraskenia', on the walls of which were engraved lists of the magistrates and other officials, as well as important records of a number of subjects. At the back of the porticos were shops, and booths, and offices.

In the centre were monuments to noteworthy citizens, and the tomb of the general – Glaukos – who was an original colonist.

A marble temple, dedicated to Zeus Agoraios stood within the walls, with a chapel, a sacrificial altar, and an adjoining circular building attached; all of which were surrounded by their own high enclosure, and foundations of all of which remain. An inscription was found on one of the pillars of the sanctuary which read 'Zeus Agoraios Thasios'. (*IG. XII. 8.*)

As so often happened Byzantine building later destroyed and ruined the earlier construction.

During the second century AD a rich Thasian named Theodectes built a complex of shops and booths with their backs supported by the back of the south-east portico.

In the southernmost corner a very large altar has been excavated, the sacrificial table measuring 2 m 74 cms × 1 m 30 cms and to the south-west of this is a row of five exedras. At least two of these monuments, which would each have contained a statue, were erected by two Thasians called Dionysodoros and Hestios. They were rich brothers who had connections with both Samothrace and Rhodes as well as other places, and also maintained a useful influence with the Roman governors of Salonica during the first century AD.

The main entrance to the agora was a great road from the southeast. This connected the centre of the city, and the all-important Passage of the *theoroi* also with the south-west approaches, from the Zeus gate, and from the Heraklion; and it would also have been the way from the Gate of Dionysos and Herakles, and from the Silenos Gate.

e great main road

edra of the sacred way (left) and detail of
ving of bucrane and rosettes (right)

On the south side of this road is an exedra which was erected during the first century BC by a Thasian called Tiberias Claudios Cadmos, a strange combination of Greek and Roman nomenclature which is of interest because of the early Kadmos connection with the island. Doubtless this man's family had friends among the Roman conquerors and possibly wished to please them.

This exedra is decorated with a frieze of garlands and bucrane for which Cadmos commissioned a local sculptor named Limendas, the son of Charapinos.

Not far from this road, in the direction of the Heraklion is a small theatre or Odeum, which may have been used as an additional theatre particularly during the Dionysos festivals, or it may have been used for musical recitals and competitions. This Odeum is roughly half-way between the Dionysion and the Heraklion. It is built of Thasos marble, and is in a good state of preservation.

During the periods of greatness enjoyed by Thasos a number of rich men undoubtedly lived there, and outside the agora, adjoining the Poseidonion, is additional evidence of this fact. Here is a residential quarter known as the 'Ground or Field of Demetriades' which was the property of a Thasian of that name, and it is known that this area was continuously inhabited for more than a thousand years, from the early Archaic period until a very late Roman epoch. Buildings of many periods are super-imposed one upon the other, with – as ever – the latest foundations largely destroying much of the earlier construction.

The Demetriades quarter is in a very pleasant part of the city, not far from the harbours, and close to the Gate of Hermes and the Charities. The ground slopes upwards towards the theatre, and is today mainly olive groves although in earlier times the slopes were covered with vines. A number of present-day Thasian citizens live in this district. Much of that which is already excavated here is in good condition, and its chief interest, apart from the quality of the stone, is the general outlay and position. Excavation in this area continues.

Odeum, or little theatre (top) and the residential quarter known as the Field of
ıetriades (below)

3

The harbours. The Acropolis: Temple of Athena
Poliouchos, Temple of Apollo, Sanctuary of Pan

Thasos had, and of course still has, the good fortune to possess a natural
sheltered harbour, consisting of an enclosed and an open port facing
to the north-west, and the whole bay is sheltered from the fierce winds
of the north-east by the Point of Evraiocastro. On this point there
are the remains of a Christian church of either the late fifth, or early
sixth century AD; and also the ruins of an ancient sanctuary dating
to the Archaic period, the exterior ornamentation of which, with its
vast blocks of gneiss, resembles one of the walls which support the
Acropolis. Much of interest was found during the excavation of this
area, including numerous votive offerings. There were also large
numbers of texts referring to Zeus, Athena, Artemis, and the Nymphs
and Kore; and there were details of the homage rendered to these
gods by the civic groups known in Thasos as *patrai*. The names here
listed of six of these groups are known – Gelontes, Priamides, Peleides,
Neophantides, Anchialides, and Amphoterides. The gods worshipped
by these groups of patrician families also had their native names such
as Artemis Orthia – possibly a Spartan influence – and Zeus Ktesios
'of the household'. The name Kore was also found on an engraved
marble in the sanctuary, and many fragments of terra-cottas and small
vases were recovered by the excavators. These had been used in the
ritual worship of this daughter-in-law of Demeter. It is interesting
that the name Gelontes is that of one of the four primitive Ionian
tribes.

The harbours have some shelter from the north-west from a small
off-shore island, and the mountains south of the city give complete
protection from the south, and east. It was noted by Jean Pouilloux
that the harbours of Thasos had given shelter to 'many a storm-tossed
traveller', and the protection of the island must have been a haven

of refuge in the days of triremes, and also of sail. Today the ferries, on which the life of the island depends, pitch and roll their way across the narrow passage from the mainland in all but the most severe gales.

The walls of the modern harbour are built on foundations which consist of the walls built during the fourth century BC, and the entrance to this harbour was made safe by a stranger named Heraklodoros, who erected two towers in recognition of help given to him by the Thasian citizens. The foundations of these towers remain, and an inscription to the above effect was found. Also found were records of the regulations concerning the numbers of ships allowed to use the harbour at any one time.

Nearer to the Point of Evraiocastro, by the modern shipyards where caiques and other boats are built on the sand, is an ancient mole running out to sea which, although now only out of the water at low tide, is plainly visible from above.

From the Point of Evraiocastro the road outside the ramparts rises approximately 135 metres to the Acropolis, passing the eastern entrance to the ancient theatre on the way, and reaching first the buildings of a mediaeval fortress built on the ruined foundations of the Temple of Apollo. This temple, dedicated to the Pythian Apollo, together with the great temple which was dedicated to Athena Poliouchos (the Protectress of the City) must have dominated the town, and must have been a magnificent sight for anyone approaching the island. Even today, when all that remains is foundations and ruins one is conscious always of these ancient strongholds of the protecting gods above the buildings of the city, the olives, and the pine trees.

Practically all traces of the Pythian have gone due to the destruction of the temple to build the fortress or great house, thought to have been the work of Byzantine engineers, because it is known that it already existed in 1259. It was later hurriedly restored by one Tedision Zaccaria between 1308 and 1318, supported by a Catalan named Ramon Muntaner, who left an account of his visit. This château was apparently finished early in the fifteenth century AD.

The Temple of Apollo was orientated north and south, and had a platform which measured 85 by 35 metres, and the construction

was entirely of marble. The foundation was partly natural, and partly reinforced, but on the eastern side – owing to the extreme steepness of the rock here – the original defences of the building are more or less undamaged. A narrow door at the southern end opens on to a small court or guardroom, to build which many of the older marble blocks were used. Outside to the north, and above a pit or cistern, is a delightful relief of a funerary banquet.

A short distance away stands all that remains of the Temple of Athena Poliouchos – marble foundations in a truly magnificent situa-

econstructed columns at
vraiocastro (facing)
funerary stele
om above the grave
t of the Temple of
pollo (right)
d remains of the
ardroom gate of the
emple of Apollo from the
st end of the Temple of
thena (below)

tion which, when the temple stood in its entirety, must have dominated the surrounding countryside and provided a focal point of real
beauty for the city below, as well as for those approaching the island
by sea.

The identification of this temple was made possible by the discovery
on the site of fragments of vases dedicated to Athena Poliouchos –
Mistress or Protectress of the City.

Athena appears in all forms of Greek art from the Archaic period
onward, and it is likely that this temple had always been dedicated
to her.

The foundations which remain are of the beginning of the fifth century BC, but there had been an earlier sanctuary on this site dating
from the first half of the sixth century BC. It is possible that the later
building was an enlargement of the older one.

The foundations consist of enormous blocks of marble which were
sealed together at the corners with 'double T' crampons or clamps.
A good illustration of this is shown below. The altar was
at the west end and faced the entrance, and the *cella* was without
colonnades but with a *pronaos*, also opening to the west. There are
also traces of the earlier Archaic building.

Many interesting objects were recovered from this temple including ex-votos of the Archaic period, bronzes, terra-cottas, and some
good pottery now in the museum.

The Acropolis bears yet another sanctuary which causes much

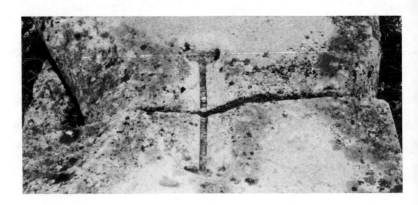

*Double 'T' crampon, Temple
of Athena (facing)
The Temple of Athena:
looking towards the entrance
(above) and part of the Naos
(right)*

The sanctuary of Pan

interest to visiting scholars. This is a simple sanctuary dedicated to the shepherd-god Pan, also much loved by the local peasants; and in *IG XII. suppl. 429* one can read that he became weary of the homage rendered to him in the Dionysion at the same time as that given to the god Dionysos – and Dionysos is here referred to as 'his master'.

Pan is an interesting study. His native land was Arcadia, and he was a god of shepherds, and flocks, and of the open air. He is at times referred to as a Son of Hermes, but he has few relationships with other gods although in Thasos he was connected with the great guardian god of the island.

His cult spread beyond Arcadia during the fifth century BC. Herodotus refers to him in Book 2, coupling his name with that of Dionysos, and also with that of the other guardian god of Thasos – Herakles – referring to all three as the youngest of the gods, but he goes on to say that in Egypt Pan was 'very ancient'. He also claims Penelope as the mother of this god, but does admit that tradition was silent after his birth until his appearance complete with horns, goat's tail and legs, and syrinx in his human hands. Brief reference is also made to Pan in Book 6.

The sanctuary on the Acropolis in Thasos is a small rock-cut shrine, to the north-west of the Temple of Athena. It stands in an olive grove, and is more or less hidden from view. It is small and simple, but the carving of the natural rock is of interest. In a semi-circular niche there is a pediment, on the left-hand part of which three goats are shown, moving forward to the call of the god's pipes. To the right, and at first seeming invisible, is the bas-relief of the god, with syrinx and *kantharos*, and above is an heraldic arrangement of another *kantharos* with leaping goats on each side of it. On both sides of the niche are offering tables for votives in the customary manner – that on the right showing clearly two drinking vessels, one of which again is a *kantharos*.

The whole of this small sanctuary has a strange charm, and the French excavators write that doubtless the soldiers of the guard on the Acropolis joined the shepherds at the sanctuary when they heard the trill of the lilting pipes.

Relief of the god Pan, within the sanctuary. The pipes in his left hand and shepherd's crook can just be made out

4

Treasures of the Thasos museum and other museums.
Pottery, local and imported

Thasos has its own museum, near the entrance to the agora, and surrounded by a garden of roses which contains an enormous statue of an heraldic bird.

Immediately within the entrance is a vast marble *kouros* of the early Archaic period – about 600 BC, which was found in the Pythion. This figure carries a ram on its right side, and the face is either obliterated, or was never carved, although the back of the head, which has long curled wig-like hair, is in excellent condition. The statue is unfinished, doubtless because of a crack in the marble near the left ear, which would have made it difficult for the sculptor to continue.

Flanking this statue on the right is the head of a horse. This is very well preserved, and is carved in realistic style. It was found during

Marble Protome of Pegasus, found in the Heraklion

the excavation of the Heraklion, and dates to approximately 460 BC. To the left of the giant *kouros* is a marble protome of Pegasus, also found in the Heraklion, in an even better state of preservation than the horse. The excavators attribute this protome to an artist working in Thasos about 500 BC.

Also found in the Heraklion is a head marked Silenus – not of a satyr – which stands at the back of the hall, and is dated to 525–500 BC. Is this the Silenus noted by Hippocrates 'who lived on the Broadway, near the place of Eualcidas ...'?

The plan of the museum is as follows:

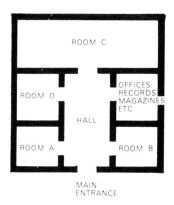

Two rooms at the front marked A and B, and a large room right across the back, marked C. On the right of the hall are small offices, records, magazines, etc., and to the left, opposite, is a room containing only Thasian pottery, marked D.

At the far end of Room A stand two interesting figures which were found in the Dionysion, where they had formed part of the sculptured decoration which carried the exedra of the Dionysion. They represent the god Dionysos, and his mother Semele, or according to some his muse. Semele is clad in a *peplos* of a design inspired by that used by the Athenian sculptor Cephisodotos for one of his most famous statues. Cephisodotos was a son of Praxitiles whose connection with Thasos is well known, and who was responsible for the most beautiful marble so far excavated in the island. This is the head of Dionysos

which crowned the central figure of the Dionysion, and is a masterpiece of early Hellenistic art.

The head is inclined to the right, and the face has a compelling
beauty – a magnetism very much in keeping with the attraction of
the cult which had gained so great a hold throughout Greece at this
time. The face is without any sign of depravity except perhaps for
the mouth which has full, rather girlish lips, and is typical of the intellectual interpretation of the god who was the inspiration of tragic
actors, and of many great artists also. This piece is well-displayed
at the entrance to Room B.

Two other statues were part of the central group; the figure of
Comedy which was found with its inscribed base which read
'Comedy – Philemon was (the) actor'. *IG. XII. supp. 400.*, and the
Mask of Tragedy, which was excavated, and is now also in Room B.

Mask of Tragedy

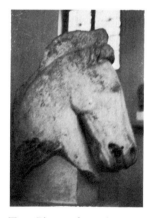

Top: Plaque, formerly part
of an altar to Cybele
Above: marble head of
horse, found in the
Heraklion
Right: figures of Dionysos
and Semele from the
sculptured decoration which
carried the exedra of the
Dionysion

Sad it is that Comedy should be without a head, and Tragedy without the body of the statue which he crowned.

A pleasing relief of Apollo and a fawn was also found in the Dionysion and is in the same room, as is a well-sculptured plaque in good condition which was part of an altar to Cybele, the Earth-goddess. It shows two gryphons mauling and devouring a deer, with a frieze of small figures above representing groups of gods. This relief was found immediately behind the museum, where a recent excavation is now uncovering some interesting buildings of the Roman era. An inscription with the plaque read '... daughter of ...ria, priestess of Cybele'. Though late, of the second century AD, it is a finely carved piece of work, and is very pleasing.

Also noteworthy, among many objects which are all of interest, is the head of a young satyr with delicately carved features which was found in the Field of Demetriades; and also a carved plaque of Aphrodite riding on a dolphin. This is of the third century BC and is of the School of Praxitiles. Of the bronzes on view far the most beautiful is a small figure of Artemis of the Archaic period which was the handle of a bronze mirror. She wears a straight skirt, and has her arms raised above her head. This little figure is in excellent condition, and is beautifully displayed by itself at the entrance to Room C.

Such gold as there is is also in Room C, although there is not very much here. There is, however, a lovely diadem in near-perfect condition, which is embossed with rosettes, lions and gryphons. There are some rings, a number of very beautifully made gold leaves with their veins carefully traced, and one or two other pieces. All the gold, as well as most of the small bronzes, was found in the Artemision, which the French concession decided to re-open for their 1976 season of excavations. Many of the pieces already found are connected with women, particularly toilet articles, jewellery, and much that is required for sewing and weaving.

It was in the Artemision also that the main local pottery factory was found, which will be dealt with later.

Ivory lions, such as those found in Palestine, in Samaria, and also in Syria, were excavated from the Artemision. These were blackened by fire, doubtless following an earthquake. The museum also displays large numbers of terra-cottas which include a delightful little figure of a comic actor, and a very large number of lamps in terra-cotta, bronze and other materials, some of which date to the Archaic period. These are displayed in the hall in front of the head of Silenus.

In Room C is an interesting sculpture of the Roman era, of Oreste and Electra, which dates to the first century AD.

At one end of Room C are the Cycladic *pinakes* (large votive plates), the best of which shows Bellerophon riding Pegasus, and slaying the *chimera* with his spear. This is of Orientalizing style, and is of the mid-seventh century BC. The *chimera* was of 'divine stock – not of men – in the forepart a lion, in the hinder a serpent, and in the midst a goat, breathing forth in terrible-wise the might of blazing fire ...' (Homer).

Thasos is indeed fortunate to have retained excellent examples of the pottery which was made in the island. A very complete picture of all types of pottery used can be pieced together from the enormous numbers of fragments excavated, and types found included much from Corinth, particularly the sub-geometric *aryballoi* (small scent bottles), Melian 'wild-goat' style pieces, as well as examples from all round the Aegean, and from Asia Minor, but the influence of the Cycladic potters in the early days was predominant. Despite the large quantity which was imported, pottery made in the island – particularly that made during the Archaic period – is of considerable interest to any student of Thasian culture.

So far the Artemision has proved the greatest source of ceramic finds, although naturally potsherds have been found throughout the island. However the local potter's workshop was in the Artemision and this was discovered in the late 1950s. This proved, beyond doubt, the existence of a considerable school of Thasian potters. Their output seems to have reached its peak during the second half of the seventh century BC, and a considerable amount continued to be made until around 570 BC, when imports from Athens which were light and elegant, as well as imports from Corinth, competed too strongly with the locally made ware, and in addition the increasing wealth of the island during the fourth century BC obviously made the purchase of imported pottery more attractive. It is also likely that some trade agreement with Athens was involved.

The workshop in the Artemision produced vases of much charm, showing animated scenes; and their colouring though rich, has a freshness, and also a certain naïvety, which in a way is more attractive than the true Orientalizing style. After the beginning of imports of Attic pieces the native potters unfortunately tried to emulate the new techniques, but inevitably the local pieces were coarser by comparison, not only from the clay used, but also in colour, glaze and brushwork, and the incision was vastly inferior, although there are a few carefully made examples. This deterioration was sad, as in its earliest stages the Thasian workshop was able to compete with imported Cycladic and other wares, until the imports of the Attic potters brought about the run-down of the island industry.

However, in the production of figurines and statuettes the island industry continued late, and there are some delightful examples extant. Nearly all the terra-cotta figures so far excavated were locally made, many of them representing either the statue of a cult, or one of the worshippers. Many of these were, of course, broken, but quite a large number were also recovered which were practically undamaged, chiefly owing to their small size. Sadly, little, if any, of the brilliant colour with which these little figures were decorated remains. One particular group of girls in tight *chitons* have the typical stylized *kore* smile on their little faces, and hold birds or flowers against their chests.

There are comic figures; satyrs; and babies crowned with pointed caps, and some female figures, seated and wearing high *poloi*. These also have the stylized *kore* smile. One or two pieces are noteworthy, in particular an ugly mask with an irregular face.

Some Black-figure pottery, made in the island, was exported to the mainland, and examples can be seen in the museum in Kavala; and pieces have also been found in the sanctuary of the Great Gods in Samothrace.

Not many vases survive although there are one or two examples

– some very large – in the museum. Large numbers of *lekanis* (plate or dish with lid) were also recovered.

To the left of the entrance hall, beyond Room A is the small room which contains only pottery made in Thasos. Here are two Black two-handled cups, very beautiful in shape and of good workmanship. They date to the sixth century BC approximately to the time when these latecomers appeared, 550–540 BC. There is one case filled entirely with perfume vials, miniature pots, and miniature bowls; and another case containing Black-figure pieces. Some of these are good, but as with much that was made by the workshop in the Artemision much was also decorated with a too-hasty brush, and therefore lacks the finish and style of Attic, and other more sophisticated potters. There are, however, some excellent examples of early Thasian pottery with a creamy-white slip, and in particular very natural flesh-tones in the slip for the figures of the fifth century. There is a large bowl with raised handles and the decoration inside, for which the potter used a very white slip; and there are two magnificent kraters. Also in this little room is a votive relief found in the Artemision, showing the head and shoulders of a woman, presumably the goddess, dating to the fifth century BC.

A large number of the carved texts found throughout the island are in Room A, most of which have been published in *IG.*, and also translated.

Reliefs of funerary banquets were a feature of the Thasian discoveries, and many of these are in a good state of preservation. These invariably depict the deceased lying on a funerary couch, often raised on one elbow, preparing to take part in the ritual feast given in honour of his death.

This is an eastern custom, and its observance can be seen in hundreds of carved or painted tombs in Egypt, and other places.

Unfortunately, as with most excavations, a number of Thasian treasures have been taken out of the island. The museum in Istanbul has a number of pieces, including the carved Herakles – as an archer – taken from the gate of the *phylakoi*. The god is kneeling on one knee, with his face turned to the left, and his head is draped with the head and front paws of a lionskin. This image appeared on some of the Thasian coins. Also in Istanbul is a fragment of the carved frieze of the proscenium of the theatre, showing Dionysos beside his panther with the last drops of wine in his *kantharos*; and part of the engraved inscription beneath, which dedicated the theatre to the god.

It is the Louvre, however, which contains some of the finest bas-relief carvings, and other pieces which were taken there by early excavators, in particular Emm. Miller. Among these treasures are the carvings from the Passage of the *theoroi*, and the fifth century BC stele of 'Philis'.

There are also Thasian pieces in private collections in Vienna, and doubtless elsewhere.

5

Famous men. Poet, painter, athlete, heroes

Not very many really famous men were connected with the island
of Thasos, but those that there were were very famous. Of these the
historian Herodotus must be of supreme importance, for without him
so much knowledge of ancient Greece and its people would be a closed
book to us. He is, however, closely followed by the great father of
medicine – Hippocrates – who lived on the island for more than three
years, and who wrote about many Thasians and their illnesses, as well
as much about the island's weather, and its vagaries of climate. His
mention of buildings in existence at that time is also of considerable
value.

Only one poet of real merit was, for a time, a citizen of Thasos
– Archilochos — the son, or grandson of the original colonizer, Telesikles.

One really great painter is known – Polygnotos – the son and pupil
of Aglaophon of Thasos, who was born in the island in approximately
470 BC.

There was a general, Glaukos, the son of Leptine; and an Olympic
athlete Theogenes, to represent the heroes.

Without doubt there were numbers of architects, artists, and arti-
sans – particularly workers in marble – who contributed greatly to
the beautiful buildings, as well as to the pottery and sculpture which
the island produced.

The wealth of Thasos also made it possible for the Thasians to
commission works from some of the most famous sculptors in Greece
during the fourth century, such as Scopas, a citizen of the colonizing
island of Paros; and Praxitiles.

Archilochos

The poet, Archilochos, is thought to have sailed to Thasos after Telesikles, with a party of mercenaries from Paros, to help resist the raiding parties of Thracians and others, and to help protect the newly-acquired city state. He was, according to Pausanias 'descended from Telesikles in the second generation'. Stephanos of Byzantium writes 'The great height of Thasos appears from the Oracle given to the father of Archilochos "Tell unto the Parians O son of Telesikles, that I bid thee found a far-seen city in the lofty isle".'

Historians and scholars, however, as well as the Thasian excavators, maintain that the original colonizer was Telesikles and that the Oracle was addressed to him, and not to his son. It is therefore uncertain whether Archilochos was his son or grandson, although grandson would seem to be the more likely. He appears to have been a wild, angry man, 'full of sound and fury', but he was unquestionably a magnificent poet at a time when poetry was truly in its infancy. Scoliasts in the 'Art of Poetry' say 'Wrath arms Archilochos with his own iambic', and he is, in fact, said to have invented the iambic metre. That he was a follower of the cult of Dionysos is shown by Marius Victorinus in the 'Art of Grammar', '... a foot less, and it will be the ithyphallic, which was invented by Archilochos, and consists of three trochees – e.g. Bacche plaude Bacche. A rhythm composed, they say, by the poet in honour of the god herein addressed.' Also in Archilochos' own words 'For I know how to lead off the pretty tune of the Lord Dionysos, my wits thunderstricken with wine ...' and again 'Each man drank from dawn onward and in Bacchic revelries ...'

Little is left of his writings, some of which are very beautiful, but the fragments, together with the descriptions of the man and his nature which remain, draw for us an oddly clear picture.

Apparently he did not have much liking for Paros – 'Heed not Paros, and those figs, and the life of the sea ...' but although he had doubtless sailed for Thasos in the hope of adventure as well as gold we soon find him writing 'How hath the misery of all Greece gathered in Thasos ...' and 'I bewail the misfortunes of Thasos ...'

He lived approximately from 712 to 664 BC, which was far from being a time of misery for the island; however, it does appear from some of the fragments of his poetry which remain, that material things were not of paramount importance with him. His main objection to Thasos seems to have been the wildness and rockiness of its country-side '... this isle stands like the backbone of an ass, crowned with savage wood ...' In an iambic poem he makes Charon, the carpenter, say 'I can not, for the wealth of golden Gyges, nor ever have I envied him; I am not jealous of the works of gods, and I have no desire for lofty despotism; for such things are far beyond my ken ...'

He apparently had an unhappy love-affair when in Thasos; he became betrothed, but did not marry. The character which emerges from his writings makes this type of affair almost inevitable, but that the fault lay partly with the girl looks possible from one of the 'Fragments'. Her name was apparently Nebule, and we read 'I would that so I might be granted to touch Nebule's hand'. Then he praises 'She rejoiced with a branch of myrtle, and the fair flower of the rose-tree in her hands, while her hair veiled her shoulders and her back ...' but later '... wretched I lie, dead with desire, pierced through with bitter pains the gods have given me ...' and also 'No longer doth thy soft skin bloom as it did; 'tis withering now ...' and '... to take a wife is patent evil ...' and then, in final despair at being supplanted by another '... the tell-tale fold of thy robe, miserable woman, showest whom thou sittest next. Delver Hipponax, he knoweth it better than any man. And Ariphanos knoweth it too ... Hipponax reft thee of thy virginity, and now all the tale's made clear ...' Horace, in the Epodes, talks of a 'tough fellow with horns, to whom the false Lycambes would not give his daughter ...' and sco-liasts written on this passage say 'he means Archilochos, who attacked Lycambes so bitterly with abusive verses that he committed suicide. Archilochos attacked him because he denied him his daughter's hand after promising it,' and later Eusthatius describes the daughter's death also by 'self-hanging'.

During a Thasian expedition to the mainland in search of Thracian gold there was a battle which the Thracians won, and in which

Archilochos was involved. With his over-preoccupation with life, and fear of death, which is apparent in 'No man getteth honour and glory of his countrymen once he be dead:... the dead getteth ever the worst part ...' unbelievably for an ancient Greek he threw away his shield, and turned and ran away. With his usual exhibitionism he boasted about this shameful happening. 'The shield I left behind because I must, poor blameless armament! What care I for that shield – it shall go with a curse. I'll get another e'en as good ...' Later, in Sparta, he was driven out of the city because of his poem proclaiming it was better to throw away his shield than to be killed. Yet, despite this incident, he was a brave man. He ended his life as a soldier '... and I shall be called a soldier of fortune like a Karian ...' His behaviour on Thasos having made the authorities only wish to be rid of him he finally returned to Paros where he was killed by a man of Naxos, named Kallondes, known as Korax, while defending his own city. Herakleides in the 'Constitutions' says of his slayer 'the poet Archilochos was killed by a man called Korax, to whom we are told the Pythian priestess gave the answer "Leave the Temple" whereupon he cried "but Lord, I am pure of ill; I slew him in fair fight ..."'

Aristotle wrote of him 'The Parians have honoured Archilochos despite his slanderous tongue.'

Archilochos was obviously a strange, violent, passionate man, frustrated and bitter, yet capable of writing beautiful poetry of which sadly so little remains. Despite all his violence of nature he must have learnt much of the lesson of life to have been able to write 'Soul, my soul, thou art confounded with hopeless troubles, look up and defend thyself against thine enemies, setting a bold front against ambushes and standing nigh unto the foe firm-planted; and exult not openly if thou prevail, nor if thou prevail not lie wailing at home; but rejoice not overmuch in delightful things, nor be vexed overmuch in ill, knowing what sort of temper possesseth man.'

Glaukos

Of the general Glaukos, son of Leptine, we have far more vague a picture, mainly drawn from the writings of Archilochos who was his friend; but there is a tomb in the agora, and the remains of cult-buildings where he was worshipped as a hero after his death.

He sailed from Paros to Thasos with the troops brought by Archilochos in the early part of the seventh century BC, and presumably he was the bandy-legged general referred to by the poet. 'I love not a tall general nor a stradling ... but for me a man should be short, and bow-legged to behold, set firm on his feet, full of pith ...' He also presumably wore his hair in the 'horn-like' bunching together fashion – 'Sing of Glaukos – the horn-fashioner ...'

During the war with Thrace – the war in which Archilochos threw away his shield – the general must also have been engaged, as the poet writes 'Look Glaukos, the waves e'en now run high ... fear cometh of the unexpected', and also 'A soldier of Fortune Glaukos is your friend until he comes to fight ...' although this could have been written at the time of the original Parian expedition to Thasos.

The funerary monument of the general is in the south-east corner of the agora, close to the Passage of the *theoroi*, and was discovered by the French School during their 1954 season of excavations, which were under the direction of M. Jean Pouilloux. There is a mnema tomb – or possibly altar – a heavy rectangle of gneiss and tufa over 4 metres long, and nearly 2 metres in width. Tufa is a stone almost unknown in Thasos, and could have been imported, possibly from the general's native island of Paros. Inscribed on a slab of marble which was inserted into the original construction, in 'boustrophedon' writing of the seventh century BC, is 'I am the tomb of Glaukos, son of Leptine. The sons of Brentes have hallowed me.' (BCH. 1955)

This is the oldest monument, and writing, so far found in Thasos.

Brentes was an obscure son of Herakles, but no one knows to whom this inscription refers, although many theories have been put forward. However the inscription proves beyond any doubt that this Glaukos is the man who was the friend of Archilochos about whom

Tomb of Glaukos – in the agora. 'Boustrophedon' writing of VII–C. BC.

'I am the tomb (or monument) of Glaukos, son of Leptinos. The sons of Brentes have hallowed (or consecrated) me.'

the poet wrote 'Such Glaukos, son of Leptine, becometh the mind of mortal man as Zeus may bring him for the day ...'

The monument is impressive for its massive construction, and particularly noticeable for its difference from the ever-present marble of most of the island's buildings. Glaukos' name appears in Paros, on the monument to Archilochos which was excavated there.

Herodotus

The 'father of History' and of all historians is a difficult subject to interpret, as although his writings tell us so much about the eastern Mediterranean lands, and their peoples, they tell us little about the man himself; although it does appear that the author of the 'Histories' had a gay and happy approach to life, which at times was almost light-hearted; and he certainly had a facile pen.

Herodotus of Halicarnassos wrote a book which was in fact a series of books, called 'Researches'. This word, translated from the Greek means *Historia*, and that great subject was created by this man, even though at times his imagination temporarily influenced some of the facts of his narrative. Without Herodotus, however, much of our knowledge would not exist, and it is salutory always to remember that he lived more than 2000 years nearer to the stories which he recorded than we do.

His date of birth is usually accepted as being 484 BC, by which time Thasos had been colonized for some 200 years. Halicarnassos was, at this time, part of the great Persian Empire – magnificent, powerful, and ruthless; and, as we have already seen, at the time of Herodotus' birth the wars which the Persians were conducting against the Greeks were just beginning to affect the Thasians.

Herodotus' apparent lack of linguistic ability – other than Greek – points to the predominance of that language in the eastern Mediterranean, and even in Egypt, and we have no indication that an interpreter accompanied him on his travels.

His 'Histories' continue to be read, despite his critics, and his obviously charming personality comes through quite forcibly. His life was short, and he died before he was sixty, leaving for posterity a book which will be used and quoted as long as books continue to be read.

Stephanos describes his tomb in the market-place in Thuria, and quotes the epitaph inscribed thereon: 'Herodotus the son of Lyxes here lies, in Ionic history without peer . . .' No confirmation or otherwise for this is forthcoming.

That he visited the island of Thasos we have in his own words ' '. . . and I have also been to Thasos . . .' and he goes on to describe a temple of Herakles built by the original settlers, whom he maintains were Phoenician.

It would appear that his stay in the island lasted for some little time, as he visited the Aliki area, and the gold-mines which were slightly further along the coast to the north-east; and he does, in fact, give a very definite description of the position of these mines, which has not to date been located. It is only lately that a road has completely encircled the island, and previously access to the south-east corner was far from easy. In Herodotus' day the journey could only have been made on foot, by pack mule, or by sea.

To quote from the 'Histories', '. . . these Phoenician mines lie between Koinyra, and a place called Aenyra, on the south-eastern side of Thasos – facing Samothrace. A whole mountain has been turned upside down in the search for gold . . .' Today there is scepticism about the existence of these mines, for few reasons other than that they have not yet been discovered. There was, one remembers, considerable scepticism about the tomb of Tut-ankh-amun . . .

The French excavators claim other mines to have existed in the west of the island, and to the present day a little gold, and other precious metals are extracted from the area near Liminaria.

Herodotus' visit, and his interest in the island, remained in his memory for a long time, and he makes several references to it throughout his books; and the famous dinner party, for which Antipaster had to pay, quoted here in chapter I, obviously took place during his stay.

Hippocrates

The dating of Hippocrates' writings is difficult, but as far as Thasos is concerned there is considerable evidence of his stay there; and he gives us many descriptions of Thasians living – and mainly dying – in the island while he was there. Plato refers to him in both the Phaedrus, and in the Protagoras. In the former Phaedrus remarks that 'Hippocrates, the Asclepiad, says that the nature even of the body can only be understood as a whole' to which Socrates answers 'Yes, friend, and he was right; still we ought not to be content with the name of Hippocrates, but to examine and see whether his argument agrees with his conception of nature ...' Most of the Thasian references are in his 'Epidemics I and III', and he lived in the island for more than three years. He was born in the island of Kos, in approximately 460 BC, and became a member of the guild of physicians known as 'Asclepiadae'. His help was sought by Perdiccas when king of Macedonia, and it was probably after this that he decided to go to Thasos.

Apart from the description of many patients, with some of whom we will deal later, he wrote much about the climate. In the 'First Constitution of Epidemics I' we read 'In Thasos during the autumn, about the time of the Equinox to near the Pleiades, there were many rains, gently continuous, with southerly winds. Winter southerly, north winds slight – droughts – on the whole winter like a spring.'

However, during the second year that Hippocrates was in the island he wrote, in the Second Constitution 'In Thasos early in autumn occurred unseasonable wintry storms, suddenly, with many north and south winds bursting into rains ... The whole year having been wet and cold and northerly in the winter the public health in most respects was good, but in the early spring many, in fact most, suffered illnesses ...' In the Third Constitution occurred for the great doctor the most interesting time that he spent in the island.

After the Dog Star, until Arcturus, hot summer. Great heat, not intermittent but continuous and severe. No rain fell. The Etesian winds blew. About Arcturus southerly rains until the Equinox. In this Constitution, during winter, began paralyses which attacked many, a few of whom quickly

died. In fact the disease was generally epidemic. In other respects the public
health remained good. As to the peculiarities of the ardent fevers, the most
likely patients to survive were those who had a proper and copious bleeding
from the nose ... For Philiscus and Epaminon, and Silenos who died, had
only a slight epistaxis on the fourth and fifth days ... Older people had
jaundice, for example Bion, who lay sick at the house of Silenos. Silenos
died on the sixth day ...

There is confirmation of the dates of certain buildings in his
reference to patients; for instance 'Pentacles, who lived near the
temple of Dionysos ...' and later '... in Thasos the Parian who lay
sick beyond the temple of Artemis ...'

The temple of Herakles is mentioned more than once, and there
is a reference to Silenos, who lived in the Broadway, near the place
of Eualcidas. This is possibly a reference to the great main road or
way, which ran from the western gates of the city past the Heraklion,
and also the Odeum, to enter the agora at the south-western corner.

Hippocrates' belief, according to his writings, was that 'Health is
held by a coction of the humours ...' and his considerable study of
the weather in Thasos is brought to bear on the illnesses which he
felt were influenced by climatic conditions.

In the First Constitution – or year – during which he lived in the
island there was obviously an epidemic of mumps, and he writes
'Many had swellings beside one ear, or both ears, in most cases un-
attended by fever, so that confinement to bed was unnecessary ...'
He refers to epistaxis, and also to jaundice, and some descriptions
are vivid in their simplicity such as 'In Thasos the woman who lay
sick by the cold water ...' The most dramatic description of a case
concerns one Crito; 'Crito, in Thasos, while walking about, was
seized with a violent pain in the great toe ... he took to bed ... at
night was delirious ... black blisters ... mad delirium ... and died
on the second day from commencement.' A close second must be 'In
Thasos the wife of Philinos gave birth to a daughter ... after fever
... delirium ..., speechlessness, she died on the 22nd day.'

Hippocrates had an obvious dislike and disapproval of excesses, as
is shown in his description of the illness of that Silenos who lived on

the Broadway. 'After over-exertion, drinking, and exercises at the wrong time he was attacked by fever ... died on the 11th day.'

It has been written that, despite the scant knowledge of Hippocrates that is left for posterity, he had become the embodiment of the ideal physician, and for those to whom the study of ancient Thasos is of importance, it is much help that he chose to spend three years of his life in the island.

Many of his 'precepts' propound his wisdom, and none more so than 'Time is that wherein there is opportunity, and opportunity is that wherein there is no great time'.

Polygnotos

At some time during the early part of the fifth century BC Polygnotos, the son, and later the pupil of the painter Aglaophon of Thasos, was born in the island. The exact date is uncertain, but it is known that he went to Athens soon after 470 BC. He later became an Athenian citizen after which he stayed mostly in the city until his death, which occurred between 445 and 440 BC.

Red-figure vase painting had, more or less, reached its limits by the time he reached Athens, and the vitality of youthful artists was turning to pastures new. Polygnotos painted murals, 'free-painting' which attempted to master both space and movement, but his knowledge of perspective could only have been of an elementary character, and he was a 'primitive', using no shading. Nonetheless, he is acknowledged as the first really great painter. His most famous work was his decoration of the Lesche of the Cnidians at Delphi, and a description of this, in considerable detail, was written by Pausanias in Book 10 of his 'Guide to Greece'. 'Above Kassotis is a building with paintings by Polygnotos; it was dedicated to the Cnidians, and the Delphians call it the Lesche (club-house). As you go into the building all the right of the painting is the Fall of Troy – and the Greeks sailing away. Menelaos' men are getting ready for the voyage; there is a painting of the ship – with men and boys among the sailors ...' Pausanias continues to give a vivid description of the whole of the painting, and ends with the words 'This is how I saw it painted by

Polygnotos'. Polygnotos painted Pandareos' daughters in this great mural, as 'grown girls, wearing wreaths of flowers, and playing with dice ...' and Pausanias says that he also brought together Odysseus' enemies on purpose.

There were some seventy figures in each of the Lesche paintings, and Simonides writes 'Polygnotos, son of Aglaophon of the island of Thasos, has painted the plunder of the fortress of Troy'.

An appreciation of stillness is shown in much Classical art, and this was apparently noticeable in the paintings of the Thasian artist. He studied in Athens with Micon, and was also connected with the circle of Cimon. Pliny accuses him of also painting little pictures of 'erotic deviations' and maintains that the Emperor Tiberius kept one in his bedroom.

The great flowering of Classical art came after the Greeks had defeated the Persians, and it is generally acknowledged that Polygnotos was its true founder, particularly with his great murals on the Acropolis, and also in the agora in Athens.

However, from the point of view of the Thasians, that part of the Delphi mural showing Tellis (Telesikles) must have been the most interesting, and in Pausanias Book 10 we read 'so Polygnotos has painted Charon as an old man. Tellis seems to be a boy in his first maturity, and Kleoboia an unmarried girl, with a box on her knees like the ones in the paintings of Demeter. I have heard about Tellis only that the poet Archilochos was his grandson, but they say that Kleoboia first introduced the secret rites of Demeter to Thasos ...' So the great painter, despite his Athenian citizenship had not, in his greatness, forgotten the island of his birth.

Theogenes

Thasos produced one great athlete, the Olympic boxer Theogenes, who won the boxing contest at the seventy-fourth Olympic Games, held at Olympia in 480 BC.

Pausanias describes him as the son of Timosthenes, a priest of the Herakles' cult, but adds that the Thasians denied that the corporal

Base of statue of Theogenes in the agora

Timosthenes was truly his father, claiming that the spirit of Herakles appeared to his mother disguised as her husband, and lay with her. Be that as it may, there is no question that the boy to whom she gave birth became a very considerable athlete. He is said to have won the pancration at the Olympics following his boxing triumph, and to have won the boxing at the Pythian Games three times. He won nine crowns at the Nemean Games, and ten at the Isthmian, divided between boxing and pancration. Later he became a distinguished runner. It is said that with all his achievements he won a total of 1400 crowns in his lifetime. Plutarch, however, puts the number at 1200, and is somewhat disparaging about some of them.

Legends abound about Theogenes, the most famous being that after his death an enemy visited the bronze statue which had been put up in his honour, and thrashed it with a whip. In Pausanias' words '...

the statue fell on him and put an end to his impertinence, but as he was killed his sons prosecuted the statue for murder, and the Thasians took the opinion of Drakon ... and drowned the statue in the sea ...' In the course of time much trouble befell the island 'the earth of Thasos ceased to give fruit' and they sent *theoroi* to consult the Oracle at Delphi. The first time the answer from the Pythian priestess was no help to the island, so they sent a second time, saying that the curse was still on the island. This time the priestess replied 'You leave great Theogenes unremembered'. The statue was eventually re-covered from the sea by some fishermen in their nets, and re-erected where it had previously stood. The Thasians re-dedicated it, and once more offered sacrifices to it as to a god, and the earth of the island recovered, and once more bore fruits in plenty.

One of the stories told about him during his lifetime was that he once ate a whole bull for a wager.

From the large number of crowns which Theogenes won it would seem likely that he not only competed in the more important games, such as Olympia and Delphi, but also in small local, possibly peasant festivals, which were held in many parts of Greece, and this would fit in with the countless rustic dramatic festivals held during the Classical and Hellenistic periods in honour of the god Dionysos.

The statue erected to Theogenes at Olympia was in the Altis – the walled enclosure of the sanctuary of Zeus – and from Pausanias we learn that the sculptor was Glaukias of Aigina. There are legends also that statues erected to this hero had power to heal the sick, but it is more likely that Theogenes himself, after his days of athletic prowess were over, became a healer.

In the agora in Thasos the sanctuary dedicated to him was too badly damaged for reconstruction, but a circular base, of marble, with three steps, is still there. This had been used for animal sacrifices made to him after his death. His statue, with its curative powers had stood in the centre of the agora, and the excavators found fragments of a list of Theogenes' victories, which had been engraved at the beginning of the fourth century BC. They also unearthed a cylindrical block of marble with an inscription of the second century BC which read:

'Whoever sacrifices to Theogenes must deposit in the offertory box an offering of first fruits to the value of at least an obole. Who does not make the deposit as stipulated will be cursed [or damned]. The money collected each year will be remitted to the *hieromemon*' [the title given to one of two deputies who were sent to the Amphictyonic Council, whose office was concerned with religious matters. In Thasos this deputy was concerned with religious finance.] The inscription continued 'This sum will be kept until the total reaches 1000 drachmae. When the above-mentioned sum has been reached, the Council and the people will meet to decide the amount of offering money, or the building will be consecrated to Theogenes with this money.'

6

Gods worshipped in the island. Zeus, Artemis, Herakles, Poseidon, and their sanctuaries

In their worship, as in so much else, the Thasian people maintained an island individuality. At many of the gates of their city were carved figures of gods, not uniformly a custom of the Greeks. High on the Acropolis stood the temples of Apollo and Athena Poliouchos. The ancient mystic religions of Demeter and Dionysos were both practised; and there is Pausanias' account of Polygnotos' painting of the sailing to Thasos of a priestess of the former cult in the original expedition from Paros. In the text of the list of divinities worshipped in the island there is a Festival of Demeter, which took place in September–October. However, no remains of her sanctuary have been discovered so far.

The cult of Dionysos flourished throughout the island, and continued late, and as considerable finds were made during the excavation of the Dionysion – which is mentioned by Hippocrates – this cult, its sanctuary, and the theatre will be dealt with in a separate chapter.

It would appear that native versions of such gods as Hermes, Hecate, the Nymphs, and the Graces were worshipped, as well as the Great Twelve who had their special festival in June–July.

At the end of the Classical period it is known that there were four attested priests in the island – those of the cults of Dionysos, Herakles, Aphrodite and Asclepios, and it is likely, though unproven, that there was a priestess of Demeter. In addition there were three *theoroi* – official representatives to the festivals of other cities, who offered sacrifices to the gods at these festivals in the name of their *polis*.

The cults of the island were doubtless those of a simple city state and, in addition to the Dionysion, in and around the agora are the remains of the sanctuaries of Zeus (Agoraios) Herakles, Artemis, and Poseidon. Zeus was the supreme god of the Olympian pantheon –

the son of Kronos and Rhea – and the only Greek god whose Indo–European background and origin can be claimed with certainty. By the sixth century BC the Greeks acknowledged twelve gods of Mount Olympos, with Zeus in command. One myth places his birth in Arcadia, and claims that the river Neda appeared suddenly to enable Rhea to wash herself and the infant after his birth. However, his chief sanctuary was at Olympia in Elis – very close to Arcadia – and here Pheidias had the workshop in which he created the famous statue of the god tragically lost to posterity, whose face is said to have come to him in a dream. Of this statue Pausanias writes 'The god is sitting on a throne. He is made of gold and ivory. There is a wreath on his head like twigs and leaves of olive; in his right hand he is holding a Victory of gold and ivory ... in the god's left hand is a staff in blossom with every kind of precious metal, and the bird perching on his staff is Zeus' eagle. The god's sandals are gold, and so is his cloak, and the cloak is inlaid with animals and flowering lilies ...' Quintilian said of this statue that it added something to human religion.

This wonderful effigy of the god was taken to Constantinople where it was destroyed by fire, in the fifth century AD.

Zeus is generally portrayed with a black beard, and as a dignified kingly figure. His loves were many and varied, and among others he fathered both Dionysos and Herakles, the two Olympian demigods. He is reported to have carried off Europa, the daughter of Aygenor, King of Tyre – whose sons Phoenix and Thasos, according to Herodotus, were among the first Phoenician colonists to visit the island of Thasos, and from whom it got its name. Book 2.45, and Book 6.47.

However, the worship of Zeus by the Thasians was the worship of Zeus Agoraios, a cult about which Professor Roland Martin wrote as the 'highest representation of the civilizing genius which so effectively aided in the formation of Greek *polis*'.

Here in the heart of the civic centre of Thasos stood a considerable temple which has been extensively excavated, and foundations, and some remains of a chapel, enclosure walls, an altar, and a circular building attached to the main temple have come to light. Good fortune had preserved an inscription on one of the columns which read '(The place of) Zeus Agoraios ...' (*IG. XII. 8.*)

The buildings had been entirely of marble, and had been part of the great re-building programme of the fourth century BC.

Only a comparatively short distance away, through the passage of the *theoroi* are the shattered remnants of the Temple of Artemis – a goddess worshipped all over Greece. A daughter of Zeus, and a sister of Apollo, it is however possible that she is pre-Hellenic. No love-affair has been recorded for her. Her proper background is the more uncultivated parts of the earth, the hills, and the forests, and particularly those parts where wild animals abound. So, in Thasos her sanctuary is above the agora and backing into the hillside, in the midst of olive and fig-trees.

There is no record still extant of either priestess or festival for this cult in the island, nonetheless the remains of her sanctuary cover a considerable area, and both priestess and festival, at some time, must have existed.

This was an older cult in the island than that of Zeus Agoraios – the Artemision was mentioned by Hippocrates during the fifth century BC, and some of the many objects recovered by the excavators date from the seventh century BC. The rituals of the cult varied, but the sacrificial animals were usually small, and often goats. Pausanias however says that game-birds were thrown alive on to the altar – surely a difficult thing to do unless their wings were bound – and that sometimes this also was done with boars and gazelles.

The sacrificial altar was also heaped with fruit, and the priest or priestess later set fire to the logs underneath it.

The sanctuary in Thasos has suffered considerable and irreparable damage, but it is possible to distinguish the general plan of the sacred enclosure. The peristyle of the main court measured 33 metres, but the entrance to the sanctuary is not easy to locate. However a long inscription was found dating from the first century BC which reads:

Whereas Epie now intends to rebuild the propylaea of the Artemision at her own expense, with marble columns, coping stones and doors – because in its present state certain openings are blocked (bricked-) up, and others are devoid of doors, it is the pleasure of the Council, and of the people, that Epie – daughter of Dionysios – should be commended for her merit, her virtue, and her generosity towards the city; and that, after the propylaea has been built she shall have inscribed thereon: 'Epie, the daughter of Dionysios, has dedicated the restoration and rebuilding of the propylaea to Artemis Eleithyia and to the people.' BCH. 1959.

A very large number of objects have been recovered from the Artemision, of which the majority were votive offerings to the goddess dating from the seventh to fifth centuries BC. Large quantities of sherds were found in the sanctuary which give a comprehensive picture of pottery both locally made and imported, which was used in the island during the Archaic period, and much of this is to be found in the local museum. The most exciting discovery made here was the sixth century BC gold headband, decorated with repoussé rosettes, and finely reliefed gryphons and lions, dedicated to Artemis.

It should be remembered that despite the proximity of the barbarian world of the east, and particularly of Thrace, Thasos remained always a bastion of Greek civilization as founded by her Parian colonizers, and the worship of the island Artemis was almost certainly the worship of the goddess introduced by them, although it is true that two dedications have been found citing Artemis Eileithyia. Eileithyia was the name of a Cretan goddess of approximately 1500 BC – the time of the Phoenician landings – as is known from the Knossos tablets, and also from Homeric poems. Undoubtedly large numbers of Thasian women bore gifts to the sanctuary above the agora, votive offerings to a goddess who must have had a reputation for help and kindness, otherwise this cult, which we know had existed from the pre-Hellenic period, would not have continued as it did until at least the first century AD, and even later.

The worship of Artemis was one of the oldest cults in the island, and proof has been found of women bearing their gifts to this sanctuary from the earliest days of the island's inhabitation. Archaic terracotta figurines, in some ways reminiscent of those placed on graves at Tanagra, have been found in the Artemision, and establish that the goddess worshipped in the island was also the Thasian manifestation of the ancient deity worshipped throughout the Aegean, and in Ionia.

A short walk westwards from the Artemision brings one to all that is left of the sanctuary of Herakles, about which there has been much scholastic argument. Herodotus claims a sanctuary of Herakles to have been built by the Phoenicians; and one of the earlier excavators – Marcel Launey – dates this temple to the time of the original Phoenician landing – 1500 BC. He claims that they founded the sanctuary, and cut the rock altar and pits, and here they worshipped Herakles as a god.

In the Archaic period, after the arrival of the colonists from Paros, another temple was built, in the form of a polygonal room (*oikos*) with an interior hearth; and here Herakles – the hero – was worshipped. Later concessions, headed by Jean Pouilloux, published excavation of the 'double' sanctuary of Herakles, as mentioned by Herodotus: to quote 'and I have also been to Thasos where I found a temple of Herakles built by the Phoenicians ... even this was five generations before Herakles the son of Amphytrion made his appearance in Greece ...' He had previously mentioned an ancient temple in Tyre 'dedicated to the Thasian Herakles'. He concludes the matter with some wisdom '... the result of these researches is a plain proof that the worship of Herakles is very ancient; and I think the wisest course is taken by those Greeks who maintain a double cult of this deity, with two temples – in one of which they worship him as Olympian and divine, and in the other pay him such honour as is due to a demi-god, or hero ...'

Certainly in Thasos there appear to have been two temples, but unhappily today the modern main road out of the city has cut through all that remains of these shattered buildings, and neither side of the road is now open to the public.

An interesting review of this subject has been published by Bergitta Berquist of Upsala University.

It is however certain that at least one temple existed at the time Hippocrates was living in the island, and this is mentioned in his Epi-

demics – third constitution. This would appear most likely to have
been for the worship of Herakles as a god, particularly as his effigy
had also been erected as a Guardian god at one of the main gates of
the city – not far distant.

Valuable finds were made in the Heraklion, in particular a protome
of Pegasos now in the museum.

The festival of the Great Heraklia was held during May–June, and
there was still an attested priest of the cult in the island at the end
of the Classical period. A part of the Archaic ritual of the cult of the
Thasian Herakles was found inscribed on a marble slab near the agora,
in the passage of the *theoroi*, which reads 'For the Thasian Herakles
the law forbids the sacrifice of a pig. The law also excludes women.
A "ninth" part of the offering is not levied. *gera* portions shall not
be cut. A price (or fee) shall not be levied.' Thasos. (*IG. XII.*) The
dating of this inscription is approximately 450 BC.

From Pausanias (V.25.12) we have a very definite description of
the worship of Herakles in the island – 'The Thasians, who were
originally Phoenicians . . . dedicated a Herakles at Olympia, with the
base and the statue both in bronze. The statue is 15 feet high, with
a club in its right hand and a bow in its left. I heard in Thasos that
they worshipped the same Herakles as the Tyrians, and then later,
when they became part of Greece, they adopted the practice of paying
honours to Herakles, son of Amphytrion as well.' This would seem
to underline and confirm the opinions of both Launey and Pouilloux
on this controversial question.

Certainly the cult was of great, if not paramount importance in
the island, and until the coming of Dionysos it is clear that the older
Herakles held first place. As in all else Thasos maintained an individual
form of worship of this god who was known to all Greeks, and who
was not unknown round the eastern Mediterranean and in Egypt.

Of the worship of Poseidon in Thasos little is known, although an
island, with its essential sea-faring inhabitants, as well as one which
had a tendency to earthquakes, must necessarily have included him
among their gods. He was an Hellenic god, one of the sons of Kronos,
and there does not seem to be any record of his earlier appearance

in the east. There is no record of an attested priest in Thasos, but there was a festival in his honour, held during December–January.

The remains of the temple, which is between the residential quarter of Demetriades and the Dionysion, is today surrounded by walnut trees, and much inhabited by bees. To the north-east is the remains of a *stoa*, and also the base of a sacrificial altar. Poseidon was not apparently thought worthy of having a temple entirely to himself, and on the north side of the sanctuary there is an altar dedicated to the goddess Hera, the wife of Zeus.

The sanctuary has a large entrance with two bays, and faces west towards the harbours. Two foundations surrounding one of the bays have been excavated, and a double consecration to Poseidon has been found, in which he is referred to as 'Lord of the sanctuary . . .' This inscription was recorded by Xenophanes, the son of Myllos, of the fourth century BC. (*IG. XII. suppl. 432.*)

In the centre of the sanctuary there is a circular base of gneiss, which could have supported another small altar.

Poseidon was worshipped throughout Ionia in historical times, and the building of a temple to this god during the Classical period would have been an obvious normal occurrence in the island.

7

The cult of Dionysos. Sanctuary, theatre, festivals. Euripides connection with Thrace and Macedonia

It has already been seen that the Thasians worshipped a number of the Greek gods of Mount Olympos, albeit in their own way, and also the two latecomers to Olympos, both born of Zeus and mortal women. Herakles has already been considered, but his fellow guardian of the city, Dionysos, also had a considerable following, and his worship in the island continued later than any other pre-Christian deity.

Many rewarding finds were made in that part of the Dionysion which it has been possible to excavate, but in addition to the sanctuary, the little theatre in the pine-trees was an integral part of the ritual of this god's worship. Both the Anthesteria, and the Choreia were held in this theatre, which must have contained a seat for the priest of the cult, doubtless carved out of marble.

The original excavation of the theatre took place at the end of the nineteenth century, but before describing what is known of this it will be helpful to consider the god with which it is connected, and as far as possible to explore the ritual of the cult as practised in the island.

Dionysos was the son of Zeus and Semele – one of the daughters of the Phoenician who became king of Thebes, Kadmos, son of Aygenor. Therefore this god was a nephew – on his mother's side – of Agave. Agave was the mother of Pentheus, who became king after his grandfather Kadmos had abdicated in his favour, and who was to be so tragically destroyed by his mother because of her utterly unreasoning and blind worship of Dionysos.

Legend has it that the goddess Hera demanded of Zeus – her husband – that he should reveal himself to Semele, whose lover he had been; or in some versions that the god coveted this woman who wished him to reveal himself to her. He appeared to her in the form of a lightning flash which destroyed her, but the unborn child was snatched from the flames and stitched until his birth into Zeus' thigh. From this unusual position, in due time, the god Dionysos was born. Some early vase-paintings tell the story, and at times a little head is shown, looking out of the god's thigh. (JHS. 1934.)

In the magnificent opening lines of Euripides' *Bacchae*, which was written between 408 and 406 BC, we have a vivid description: 'I am Dionysos, the son of Zeus ... come back to Thebes, the land where I was born. My mother was Kadmos' daughter, Semele by name – midwived by fire, delivered by the lightning's blast ...'

Praxiteles statue of the god Hermes, carrying the infant Dionysos to the care of the nymphs of Mount Nysa. In the museum at Olympia.

To account for this god the Greeks describe Hermes taking the baby Dionysos to the nymphs of Mount Nysa – somewhere far to the east. His origin is, in fact, often referred to as Phrygian, and sometimes as Lydian. The Phrygians were a Thracian tribe who had emigrated in an easterly direction in approximately 1200 BC, and were believed to have overthrown the Hittites. Praxitiles' famous statue at Olympia shows Hermes carrying the baby Dionysos on his left arm. There is a certain likeness, particularly of the nose and forehead, between the face of the Praxitiles' Hermes and the marble head of Dionysos attributed to Praxitiles which was excavated from the Thasos Dionysion. In the Museo Etrusco Gregoriano is a calyx krater dated approximately 435 BC, which is painted with a picture of Hermes arriving on Mount Nysa with the infant Dionysos, and there are also later paintings showing him being brought up by nymphs and maenads. The satyrs of Mount Nysa helped the nymphs in the young god's upbringing, and as he grew in years so the *thiasos* – the revel rout of satyrs, maenads and other worshippers – developed. Finally he came from the east, from Phrygia or possibly from Thrace, making a triumphal entry into Greece attended by his followers; a dangerous and wildly attractive deity.

The cult was, in the main, an emotional religion; and the god was more the god of fertility and re-generation than of wine. In fact some scholars particularly emphasize that he was the god of souls. All fruits, and corn were connected with the early Dionysos, and only later did he become more associated with wine.

An early cult-figure and shrine of an Asiatic Dionysos was found in Brusa, and details were published by Haspels – an account of which appeared in the JHS. The figure was large with a damaged face and was wearing a short pleated *chiton*. It had a bunch of grapes hanging from either side of its head, a *kantharos* in the right hand, and a staff in the left. Each side of the god were rearing snakes' heads. A second figure of coarse grey marble had a plain *chiton* with a *nebris* over it, and was holding a bunch of grapes in its right hand, and a staff in the left. A satyr stood to the right of this figure, with goat's horns and ears. According to Haspels these are typical of votive statues found to the north-east of Türkomen-Dăg, and point to a very special Dionysiac cult on the north-east side of the Phrygian highlands. Haspels also maintains that the figures were brought to the coast by the Greeks in 1921–1922.

Early vase-paintings show an elderly Dionysos with a black pointed beard. In the Archaic period he is mostly represented as a dignified god with a beard. He carries the *kantharos*, and sometimes the *thyrsos*, a giant fennel stem topped with ivy. Later he is always younger, generally beardless, and frequently wearing a panther-skin, or even riding the panther. He still carries the *thyrsos* and often holds the *kantharos* in his other hand. Sometimes he is accompanied by his attendant satyrs and maenads, or is with Semele, or with Ariadne who became his wife after Theseus deserted her on the island of Naxos. By the Hellenistic period the face is intellectual, gentle, and almost serene.

Homer, with his intense concentration on heroes and heroic deeds, makes only brief mention of Dionysos, noting his birth, and recording an unattractive incident of the god taking flight and seeking refuge under the sea. However there is no question that the worship of this god spread rapidly throughout Greece, and lasted for a very long time – a violent religion with a very powerful attraction.

By the fifth century BC the cult in Attica and in southerly parts of Greece had changed, and in some ways had lost the more extravagant aspects of its ritual, although it still exercised considerable power over its followers. There had, however, been opposition in certain places, particularly in Thebes. Here the king, Pentheus, had met with a disastrous fate when endeavouring to oppose the powerful 'stranger'. The earliest illustration of the death of Pentheus was painted about a hundred years before Euripides wrote the *Bacchae*. In this painting the body of the king is being torn and dismembered by ecstatic and infatuated women, in an access of irrational emotional stimulus. (Attic Red-figure Vase-painters – Beazley.) There is also the well-known painting in the House of the Vettii at Pompeii, which shows Pentheus being torn to pieces by maenads. The original of this was painted during the first half of the fourth century BC, but the extant copy is about AD 70.

By the end of the fourth century BC in Macedonia and in Thrace – the background to which Thasos belonged – the god and his cult were still more primitive in form – in some ways purer, and more miraculous in ecstasy than was possible in the now more civilized south. It is thought that the ritual was wilder, and, seen from the distance of time, more horrifying in its form. Sacrifices in the north at any rate were still '... first a goat, then a number of larger animals, then a man ...' Dionysos was indeed the god of wine, but he was also the god of nature; and of the beauty, majesty and overwhelming truth of the primitive in both man and nature. He was a god of music, and also a god who could inspire an all-possessing ecstasy – lifting man out of himself to meet the demands of an absolute and engulfing worship. To quote again from the *Bacchae* Dionysos in his own words very simply describes himself 'and he shall know Dionysos, son of Zeus – in his full nature god, most terrible, although most gentle to mankind ...' As a god he could bring rapture to men, and also the deepest anguish. Once more to let Euripides describe this worship – in the second Strophe of the *Bacchae*:

Blessed blessed are those who know the mysteries of god,
Blessed is he who hallows his life in the worship of god, he whom the spirit of god possesseth, who is one with those who belong to the holy body of god.
Blessed are the dancers and those who are purified, who dance on the hill in the holy dance of god.
Blessed are they who keep the rite of Cybele, the Mother.
Blessed are the Thyrsus-bearers, those who weald in their hand the holy wand of god.
Blessed, blessed are they. Dionysos is their god.

This was written in 407 BC at the height of the cult which had swept through the whole of Greece in the seventh and sixth centuries BC, and remained, particularly in northern Greece and Macedonia, for many hundreds of years later than this.

Dionysos is said at times to have shared Apollo's shrine at Delphi, although these two gods represented totally different aspects of the Greek nature. However there were likenesses in their backgrounds. Both, for instance had an ancient cult in Crete; and in a tale told by Pindar about the shrine of Asclepius at Epidaurus Apollo had snatched the body of Asclepius from the dead body of his mother in much the same way that Zeus had snatched the infant Dionysos from

Semele. On a vase-painting which shows the sacred enclosure at
Delphi Apollo is giving his right hand to Dionysos, which obviously
shows a pact between the priests of the older cult and the new.

The *dithyramb* – inseparable though it is from Greek tragedy – was
nonetheless a Dionysos cult-song, and its true origin is unknown,
although mention of it is made by Pindar, and its possible origin was
written about at some length by Herodotus. It is thought to have been
chanted by a *coryphaeus* (leader) and a chorus, and is in fact mentioned
by Aristotle in his *Poetics*. Herodotus' account is worth quoting,
although the *dithyramb* had existed as a cult-song considerably earlier
than his account of it. '. . . it concerns Arion of Methymna – the most
distinguished musician of that date – and the man who first, as far
as we know, composed, and named the *dithyramb* – and trained choirs
to perform it in Corinth.' There follows the well-known story of
Arion and the dolphin.

In the *Bacchae*, written some eighteen years after the death of Herodotus we have the choral song in action. When Dionysos, disguised as
the 'Stranger' is led away captive at Pentheus' command, in Euripides'
words the chorus chant:

> O Dirce, holy river
> Child of Archelaös' water
> Yours the spring that welcomed once
>   divinity, the son of Zeus!
> For Zeus the father snatched his son
>   from deathless flame, crying
> Dithyrambus, come!
> Enter my male womb
> I name you Bacchus, and to Thebes
> Proclaim you by that name.

Thasos reached her original period of greatness during the seventh
century BC, which was a time of true economic prosperity and some
cultural magnificence for the island; and again, after some long time
of misfortune, rose to a high peak of prosperity and civilization during
the fourth century BC. The island could not but be influenced by the
strongest cult on the nearby mainland, where in any case its colonies

were situated, although as always the islanders retained a certain individuality even in their worship. There was still an attested priest of Dionysos in Thasos at the end of the Classical period – about 330 BC, and it is reasonable to assume that this was so as long as the cult remained active in the island.

Dionysiac rituals were varied, and were mainly based on fertility, re-generation, and the things of nature, but it does appear that the Thasian cult was ecstatic and maybe mystic, rather than orgiastic. This was so at any rate after the revival of independence and prosperity during the fourth century BC. During the Classical and Hellenistic periods Dionysos is represented as the intellectual inspiration of artists and actors, and in particular as the god of the theatre, and of the tragic actor, and indeed of tragedy itself.

Herodotus claims that the names of all the gods came from Egypt, and describes at some length the rituals employed there; and he also claims an original appearance of Dionysos – according to Egyptian reckoning, in these words: '... and even Dionysos, the youngest of the three [Pan, Herakles, and Dionysos] appeared they say 15,000 years before Amasis ...' Amasis' dating, according to Manetho, with his 'nine kings of Sais' was 570–526 BC, which if correct would put the origin of the cult at approximately 15,550 BC. It is impossible either to confirm or deny this statement. However, the most likely date for the appearance of the cult on Thasos is at some time during the early Parian occupation of 680 BC. We may not know exactly when this cult was first practised in the island, but we do know that it continued late. In the Roman epoch there were several Dionysiac 'associations' on Thasos, and it was for one of these that a doctor named Timocleides laid out a little sanctuary during the first century AD. In it was found the following dedication:

For you a temple open to the sky enclosing an altar, and an arbour of vine branches, O Prince of the Maenads; a beautiful lair which is always green. Here Dionysos Bacchos this is set up for you by Timocleides, son of Diphilos – And for the initiates an ancient *oikos* (small building) in which to sing Evohé – And a clear flashing stream for the nymphs, with your blessing, to mix with that so sweet nectar which takes away the cares of men – and this is consecrated to your ministry O blessed one – and you, in your turn keep a doctor on Thasos, his native land, to keep it safe and sound – You who return to us always young, year after year.

Martin Nilsson, in his 'Dionysiac Mysteries of the Hellenistic and Roman Age' refers to 'family associations' on Thasos, and describes in some detail the type of buildings and grottos used, as well as the dining couches. The Latin word for these was *stibadium*, which one of the earlier French excavators maintains was either a building, or an exedra.

According to the records (taken from the texts) three festivals of Dionysos were celebrated in the island; the Anthesteria, the Dionysia, and the Choreia. The Anthesteria, throughout Greece, was the most important of the Dionysiac festivals – with the possible exception of the great City Dionysia held annually in Athens – and was held during the month Anthesterion (January–February). During the Anthesteria the god was ritually re-united with the dead, from which the mytho-logical likeness to Osiris is apparent. The festival also celebrated the opening of the new wine. The great ceremony of unsealing took place on the first day, and the tasting on the second day. At the tasting it was an essential part of the ritual that everyone, even children, should bring his own drinking vessel, called a *choes* jug. Choes was also the name of the second day of the festival, and this custom had arisen from the day of Orestes' visit to Athens after his matricide, and before his purification, when the priest insisted that everyone should use his own jug to escape pollution. Many thousands of these *choes* jugs have been found near the sanctuaries of Dionysos all over Greece.

On the second day also there was a ritual marriage between the god and his priestess – the part of the god generally being performed by the husband of the priestess. There was also a drinking contest, and all was accompanied by singing and dancing which at times carried the celebrations to considerable excess. All the cult-objects, such as *thyrsoi*, fawnskins, masks and so forth were in use, and wreaths of ivy were worn by those taking part. On the third day the *panspermia* was cooked, which was a mixture of fruits and seeds prepared in special pots known as *chytroi*, thus underlining the fertility and regeneration aspects of the cult.

The Dionysia was held during the known month Thasian–Galaxion (March–April) at a time when the rainfall was usually slight. The actors were always masked, and the mask was, in fact, a cult-object, frequently hanging on a pole beside the cult-statues in the sanctuary.

The Thasian Dionysia doubtless followed in a simple way the type of rustic festival held in villages and towns all over Greece, and should not be confused with the Great City Dionysia which was held annually in Athens in the theatre below the Acropolis, to award the tragic prizes for the year. The City Dionysia originated during the second half of the fifth century BC, when a tragedy by Thespis was performed, and the stone seat erected for the priest of the Dionysos cult can still be seen on the Athens Acropolis site. However, for centuries after the City Dionysia had come to an end, the theatres of Dionysos throughout Greece were a setting for drama, in particular for the plays of the great tragedians, and later also for comedy.

In Thasos the site of their Dionysia was naturally the theatre, although the ceremonies doubtless started in the temple.

Singing and dancing were a part of all Bacchic festivals. Herodotus, in Book 8 refers to the 'Iacchos' song being sung at all the Dionysiac mysteries, and Euripides, in the *Bacchae* mentions the dancing when Pentheus asks: 'Is Thebes the first place you have introduced this god?' and the 'Stranger' replies 'No! Every eastern land dances these mysteries'.

Both the snake and the *thyrsos* were used in Bacchic dances, and the former played a prominent part in the earlier Phrygian cult, the cult sometimes known as that of the 'divine child'.

In the Thracian version however the god was very frequently represented as an animal 'First the goat . . .' and as such was torn to pieces and eaten by his worshippers. Mention is constantly made of the followers of Dionysos eating the god when represented by an animal.

The third festival, the Choreia, took place shortly after the Great Heraklia, in the known month Thasian Thargelion (May–June) and this also took place in the theatre.

No one has better described the magnetism of Dionysos than Professor Albin Lesky, in his well-known book on Greek tragedy:

Not prayer and sacrifice alone satisfies Dionysos – man's relationship with him is not the reciprocity of giving and receiving that is so often cool and calculating. He demands the whole of man, ravishes him, submits him to fearful ritual, lifts him in ecstasy above the cares of the world. That he should be the god of wine expresses only one aspect of his being, which encompasses all the urgent passionate life of nature, all its creative potencies. In his orgiastic service Nature itself releases man from the problems of existance, draws him into the deepest realms of its mystery, the mystery of life itself. (*Greek Tragedy* – Lesky.)

The Thasian sanctuary of Dionysos has proved to be one of the most rewarding sites of the excavations, although unhappily much of it is still covered by modern building. Only a part of the whole sanctuary is free of the houses in which Thasians of today are living, and most of the temple of the god, built as it was on the western side, is impossible to excavate – at any rate at the present time. However, in the north-eastern area much of value has been recovered. All that is so far known of the main sanctuary is that there were at least two entrances, one to the west, and one to the north-west; it is also known that the foundations of the court were built of blocks of marble. marble.

At the north-eastern corner the base of a monument has been discovered on which stood the cult-figures of the tragic Dionysos of the theatre, some of which have been recovered; and in addition two more figures were found – that of Dionysos, much draped, but with the panther-skin on his left shoulder – and a female figure draped in a *peplos*, said to be Semele.

The cult-figures in the sanctuary stood in a semi-circle, with the god to the right of the other figures (see plan). Next to him was the mask of Tragedy, then the heavily-draped figure of Comedy. Then came the Dithyramb, and lastly the figure which represented the Nocturnal Serenade. These figures were dedicated at some time during the Hellenistic period, to commemorate a season of theatrical productions.

The building in which the base of these statues stood faced a porch of four Doric columns, up to which led a long flight of steps. Two

Dionysion. The inner sanctuary

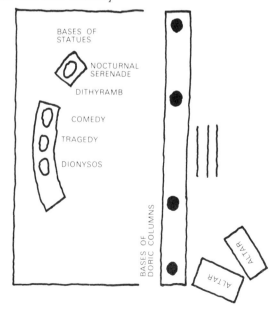

BASES OF
STATUES

NOCTURNAL
SERENADE

DITHYRAMB

COMEDY

TRAGEDY

DIONYSOS

BASES OF
DORIC COLUMNS

ALTAR

ALTAR

altars can be seen to the left of the staircase. The older of these was made of slabs of marble and gneiss, with a sunken hearth, and was used for sacrifices to invoke the Good Spirit (Agathos Daimon). This altar had originally been in use in Archaic times. The other, which is of the fifth, or early fourth century BC, is of the type known as *in antis*, with an offering table, and two pillars – made of marble tiles. The beautiful marble head of the god, either by Praxitiles or his school, which was found in the sanctuary, belonged to the statue which presided over the grand exedra of the Dionysion.

Hippocrates mentions the Dionysion in his Epidemics, when referring to a patient called Pentacles, in the Third Constitution.

No one can know what treasures wait to be brought to light in the temple under the houses.

From the Dionysion a flight of wide marble steps leads upwards to the theatre in the pine-trees – to enter through, what should be, the western gate. On this western gate was found a bas-relief decoration, and an inscription, but these have been removed. However there is a record of the votive inscription which was offered by a superstitious mariner after a safe voyage. He is reconciled to Nemesis, but does not boast of his good fortune as it was forbidden to invoke Agathe Tyche (good fortune). A record of this inscription was published in the JHS of 1887.

The theatre is set in a natural hollow some 100 metres above the town, and is overhung with aromatic pines. From all sides are beautiful views, although not from the orchestra itself. There are some interesting notes about the original excavation, published by E. J. Hicks, and J. Theodore Bent in the JHS of 1887 – a copy of which was presented to the Society of Antiquaries of London in 1888. At this time almost the whole theatre was covered with brushwood and soil, but the lines of the seats were visible; and also the colonnade behind the stage, although whether at this time there were more columns which were later removed is uncertain. Apparently there were some thirty rows of seats under the soil, and between the seats and the orchestra there had been a wall made of blocks of marble. Most of these blocks

Dionysion: marble steps approaching the sanctuary and base of cult-s▪

had been pushed forward into the orchestra by a movement of the soil, probably caused by a slight earthquake shock; and some of them were already missing. Most of those remaining were inscribed. In the same issue of the JHS is a report of the considerable alterations made by the Romans during the first century AD, who, among other things, partially destroyed the elegant colonnade behind the proscenium.

The orchestra was paved with marble, and a narrow passage by which the chorus entered ran under the stage. There was a Doric colonnade between two pilasters supporting the proscenium, and behind this the bases of six massive columns were found.

The Thasian, Lysistratos, son of Codis, dedicated the proscenium to the god Dionysos, and this has been reconstructed on a plan by the French excavators. A copy of the dedication can be found in *IG. XII. suppl. 339.*

Only one pillar and part of another remain, and some small pieces of the *metope*, although a certain amount of the frieze survives, with some part of the dedicatory inscription, and is in the museum in Istanbul.

From the writings of Hippocrates we know that a theatre was in use during the fifth century BC, and doubtless it was built, or re-built during the great programme of reconstruction which took place during the fourth century BC.

The Thasian Hegemon both wrote for, and acted in the Thasos theatre, possibly in the first comedy ever produced there.

After the arrival of the Romans it was altered – and degraded – into a gladiatorial arena, the orchestra being changed by the erection of heavy doors to obstruct the *paradoi*. It was said that a son of Dionysos was one of the gladiators who took part in the contests, and performed fantastic feats in the arena.

Today it is pleasant to walk up a path outside the walls, starting near the Point of Evraiocastro, with magnificent views of the sea through the trees all the way, and to enter the theatre from above. The path continues to the Acropolis, and the great temple of Athena Poliouchos, the Protector of the City.

Doubtless unknown to most of the citizens of Thasos at the time of the reconstruction of their city, one of the greatest of the Greek

*The theatre (above)
and an inscription
found there (left)*

The Theatre

Modern buildings above the sanctuary of Dionysos, covering a large part of the temple site

tragic poets – Euripides – was born. The exact date is not known, but the Parian Chronicle gives it as 484 BC.

He was the son of a landed proprietor although there are many contrary versions of his background, and he was born on his father's estate at Salamis; and not, as is so often written, at the time of the battle of that name. As frequently happens with work which is really great, his poetry was not valued at its true worth until after his death. Not until 455 BC did he manage to get a Chorus, and his *Peliades* won him a third prize in 441 at the City Dionysia. It is thought that by this time a number of his ninety-odd plays must have been written. However, a few years before he died, the king of Macedonia – Archelaus – summoned him to the brilliant, intellectual court at Pella, to which the capital had been moved, and to which the king either invited, or attracted many philosophers, writers and artists from Athens, and from other parts of Greece. Euripides had never really been happy in Athens, although he numbered many sophists, and philosophers among his friends. He had been late in winning a prize, and he must have suffered considerable disillusion, and doubtless frustration in the great city towards the end of his life. When the summons from Archelaus came he at once moved to Pella, some say into voluntary exile. It is, however, more likely that he was attracted by the greater freedom of Thrace and Macedonia, and by the erudite group who surrounded the king. Here, during the last three years of his life he wrote three plays; the *Archelaus*, which has been lost; *Iphigeneia in Aulis*, and his last, and undoubtedly his finest play, the *Bacchae*, both of which

'soft boots of the
tragic actor

Ancient Pella

Dionysos on panther.
Mosaic from museum
at Pella

survive. We have evidence that the cult of Dionysos was practised in Pella from a late fourth century BC pebble mosaic of the god, riding on a panther, which is now excavated and preserved in the museum there.

The *Bacchae* was written in 407 BC, although it may have been in preparation before this. Euripides died in 406 BC.

Written as it is entirely round the person of the god Dionysos, the *Bacchae* is of incomparable value to modern understanding of this powerful religion. No other Greek god or goddess has so complete a contemporary account written about him or her, or about the rituals and practices of their cults. One of the more interesting aspects of the play is that Euripides insists that his maenads were pure; and this we must accept. His herdsman, in a magnificent speech tells Pentheus: '... but modestly ... not as you told us, drunk with wine' and again 'they were a sight to marvel at for modest comeliness ...'

However Dionysos had also gathered into his *thiasos* a number of satyrs – those mythical creatures who had assisted the nymphs of Mount Nysa in his upbringing, and at the Gate of Silenos, which is the main exit from the town of Thasos inland to the island, there is a superb relief of one of these wanton creatures who so vividly represent all that is reckless and passionate, as well as uninhibited in nature. The figure is ithyphallic, with a long tail, which proclaims a horse – rather than a goat – satyr, it carries a *kantharos*, and wears the soft boots of the tragic actor. The link between Dionysos and tragedy is indissoluble, and this is again emphasized by the soft boots worn by many of the satyrs. The face of the figure at the Silene gate is very worn, but it appears also to be wearing the Mask of Tragedy. There is no way of proving that Euripides visited Thasos, although it has been said that he wrote part of the *Bacchae* on the island. Pella was, at this time still on the sea, with its own harbour, and the island of Thasos – then under the protective cloak of Macedonia – only a short sail away.

The plays of Euripides have been performed continuously in the island's little theatre, as well as those of other Greek tragic poets, and there is an annual festival held there to this day.

8

The Texts. Passage of the theoroi, organization of the life of the city from the texts

The fourth century city of Thasos was well organized and well governed, and many lists of laws and of officials of the city have been found at Evraiocastro and other places, and also in the most controversial and in many ways the most interesting discovery yet made by archaeologists – the Passage of the *theoroi*.

Theoroi – in Thasos eponymous magistrates – were representative of the various cults practised, and were much used as religious ambassadors to various places, and in particular to Delphi. They served under the Archons, the supreme rulers of a city, but ranked next to them for all purposes other than religious. In religious matters their opinions and rulings were undisputed.

Originally the *theoroi* – the word means 'observers' – were travellers, and attendants at festivals given by far-off cities, but later became envoys who announced coming festivals and celebrations of the Games. They were, naturally, sacred messengers as all Greek games were of a religious nature. Little by little the religious life and functions of the *theoroi* became more and more important until by the fourth century BC, the title was given to religious magistrates who were elected annually.

It is known that towards the end of the Classical era there were three *theoroi* in the island representing all the cults, and doubtless forming a religious council with the attested priests. The *theoroi* of Thasos also continued to be travelling delegates to religious centres, such as that of the Great Gods of Samothrace.

Despite all this there were eighteen religious festivals held in the island each year, doubtless of a simple nature, but worshipping at least ten of the gods, and at a later date the king Alexander the Great, and many of the local Thasian heroes.

A list of the holders of religious office was found inscribed on the west wall of the Passage of the *theoroi*, with the names in groups of three.

In 1863 one of the earlier travellers to the island – Emm. Miller – who would today be designated as a treasure hunter rather than an archaeologist, found this passage and partially excavated it. He described his ideas beforehand, saying that he would find a 'long square room', supported by pillars at the corners connected by a wall. The pillars would also be square. There would be no door.

In fact the excavation revealed a passage with marble walls measuring 11 metres in length, with pilasters at each end. It was approximately $3\frac{1}{2}$ metres high. This passage, possibly the most important of the whole excavation of the ancient city, is at the south-east angle of the agora outside the north-east and south-east porticos, and was built in or about 470 BC.

Miller, unfortunately, found three superb bas-reliefs which will be described later, tore them from their positions and took them to the Louvre, leaving no record of exactly where they had been sited, or other essential details of their discovery. The inscribed list of religious magistrates, which was also removed, dates from the end of the fourth century BC, and was doubtless put up during the great re-building programme. The names were grouped in threes in the usual manner.

Unfortunately we do not know, nor ever shall, the exact function of this sacred passage.

A deep niche in the south-east wall contained an altar, and it was from this niche that the three reliefs were removed and taken to the Louvre where they can be seen in the Parthenon room. They represent Apollo and the Nymphs; Hermes, and the Graces.

The largest of these is a fine bas-relief showing Apollo with his lyre being crowned by a Nymph or attendant – some say Peitho – who wears a *peplos* of Doric style. On the right is a group of three nymphs in procession carrying their offerings to the altar. In the centre is a niche – argued by some to be a false door – which could have contained a cult-statue. Above the niche the cult-ritual is inscribed: 'To the Nymphs, and to Apollo (of the Nymphs) sacrifice a male or female

Entrance to passage of the theoroi

at your will. It is not permitted to sacrifice neither sheep nor pig . . .'
(*IG. XII. 8.*)

On the east wall of the sanctuary some of the native gods of the
city awaited the arrival of the visiting gods to whom the colonists
of Thasos had paid tribute, in particular the Pythian Apollo.

In the centre was an altar standing in a large recess, and to the right
of this recess stood the god Hermes – the 'silver-tongued Messenger
of Olympos', in his native guise.

He stands with right hand stretched forth inviting sacrifice on the
altar, and is clad in a short pleated mantle, and pointed hat; and he
holds the *kerykeion* in his left hand. Behind him stands a female figure
– maybe Hecate – who carries a coronet or crown. The instructions
for the sacrifice are brief: 'It is not permitted that the Graces sacrifice
either goat or pig.'

The bas-relief of the Graces was apparently on the opposite side
of the altar, and these three figures, in pleated *pepla* have their left
hands raised, bearing offerings for the sacrifice. One of them is bearing
a coronet.

Hermes was a god well-known in Thasos. Accompanied by his
attendant Graces he had his own carved gate; and there is also a votive
bas-relief of the four which was excavated, and is now in the museum.
The clothes of this group are of the Ionian Archaic period, but the
execution is later.

There are various points of interest in these reliefs and it is indeed
unfortunate that Miller could not have left them in situ.

The arrangement of the largest – that of Apollo – was placed on
one side, and two smaller engravings, flanking an altar, on the other.
This is the same design as the *phylakoi* gate, where on one side was
the large carved block of the Dionysiac *thiasos*, and on the other the
two smaller reliefs of the guardian gods, Dionysos and Herakles.

The instructions for sacrifice are difficult and appear to oppose each
other – 'neither pig nor sheep – nor pig nor goat'. Yet there is only
one altar between the two, and it is known that access to this was
not a permanent structure. Is it possible that here the priests of the
two cults sacrificed from opposite positions? Presumably the priest

of each cult sacrificed at different times. This point also remains un-resolved. There is, however, a lesson to be learned from such a place of dual worship which is said to be unique in Greece, as it is un-doubtedly indicative of the religious adjustment necessary for the Greeks who founded this island colony in Thracian territory.

Another altar was found near the most northern point of the east wall, and an inscription was also found engraved near its foundation which indicated that it was dedicated to Athena Propylaia.

Offering tables had been arranged along the east wall, and one of these was dedicated by the *apologoi* – the magistrates for justice – to the goddess Hestia, the representative of family life among the Olym-pians, and who 'liked not the works of Aphrodite'.

Yet a third altar has been excavated at a level indicative of the late Roman period.

The position of the Passage is of supreme importance studied in the context of the religious life of the city. Immediately to the north lies the agora, with its Temple of Zeus, and cult buildings to Thasian heroes to whom sacrifices were offered after they died. To the south, adjacent to the entrance of the passage, is the Artemision, and only a very short distance east is the all-important Dionysion. From the west end of the Passage it is only a short distance to the Great Main Road or Sacred Way, which leads to the Heraklion, and on to the Zeus Gate.

There were other sanctuaries in the city as yet waiting to be exca-vated, and these could also have been in the same area, which is now very much built over. There was an attested priestess of Aphrodite, and a priest of Asclepios, as well as a priestess of Demeter as painted by Polygnotos, and cult-buildings and altars for these gods must have existed.

On the north-east side of the agora is another building to which importance is attached for the engraved lists and records which it con-tained. This building ⊣▭⊢ and resembling the Zeus portico in the agora in Athens, is over 21 metres long, by 9 metres wide. Un-fortunately here again Byzantine building has ruined the original structure except for its foundations, and the eastern angle.

Built entirely of marble it stood against the northern end of the north-east portico, which contained shops, stalls and booths. The marble colonnade of this building was of Doric columns, and winged laterals jutted out at the sides.

The dedication had been engraved on the architrave, but only two letters (TI) of the inscription could be deciphered.

A row of statues had stood in front of the façade, the bases of which remained, and the building dated from the fourth century BC.

Here had been the administrative centre of the city, and here were engraved the names of the Archons – the magistrates who governed the city – who were elected annually. This list was complete from the middle of the fourth century BC, until the third century AD. Here also had been inscribed official communications from Rome, decisions of the Senate, and letters from Claudius and Nero.

The building stood until the fifth century AD, when it was destroyed to enable a Christian edifice to be erected on the site.

9

Gold. Marble. The quarries at Aliki, and the sanctuary there. Coins. Wine

Much has been written about Thasian gold from Herodotus onward, and the area of Kinyra – of which the historian wrote '... and these Phoenician mines lie between Koenyra, and a place called Aenyra, on the south-eastern side of Thasos, facing Samothrace ...' – is today generally accepted as the most likely place for the ancient mines to be.

Thasian gold is also briefly mentioned by Thucydides, in Book 4 of the 'Peloponnesion War', although this may refer to those mines on the mainland of Macedonia, owned by Thasos, which fact is not disputed.

Kinyra has a particularly beautiful bay, and there is a small village of less than fifty houses constructed of marble with marble slates for the roof. Nearly all these houses are built along the edge of the shore, and olive groves almost cover them from the landward side. The mountains rise steeply above, to a height of over 3000 feet, with many crags and pinnacles. The lower slopes are covered with cistus maquis, and some fine flowering trees. A small island lies offshore, which is also called Kinyra. As this name is of Semitic origin it would seem likely that at some period there were Phoenicians in this part of the island.

So far, there has been little excavation in this area, and no trace of the mines has appeared, although one hears talk of peasants panning for gold in the mountain streams, and even of minute quantities being recovered, but this is unproven. Modern geologists are sceptical, but there are some modern scholars who think that the presence of these mines is not impossible.

Traces of a sanctuary of Herakles Melqart found here also underline an early Phoenician occupation of this part of the island. In any case it would appear impossible absolutely to discount the possibility, particularly as there are other mineral deposits in the island, notably in the south-western district. Iron is extracted from the country inland of Cape Kephalas, and from this source came the fortune of the little town of Liminaria. There is known to be silver in Thasos, and the Thasian's early coinage was minted with silver from their own mines, but the south-eastern area where the gold is supposed to be is extremely difficult of excavation, and any such enterprise would be very costly indeed. Possibly, one day, gold in real quantity, will make its appearance in one of the island's torrential streams.

There can be no argument about the existence of marble in the island – it is everywhere. The quay in Thasos town is paved with it; many of the houses are built of it; and the roads and paths are strewn with marble chippings.

The main quarries are in the Aliki neighbourhood, and the modern road runs beside them for some miles. Marble carrying boats are frequently to be seen in Thasos bay, as it is easier to load from the quay there, but they also lie off Aliki from time to time. Quarrying has taken place at Aliki since the sixth century BC, and the process continued without interruption until the Roman era.

Under the Romans the industry was considerably increased, as Thasian marble was in great demand in Italy for which there is much evidence – (Plutarch, Pliny, Pausanias). The Sanctuary of the Great Gods of Samothrace, on that island, was built of Thasian marble, as were naturally all the temples and other great buildings in Thasos itself.

Above the handful of old-type Thasian houses which huddle round the two bays of Aliki is a large area of glittering white marble, but the ancient quarries were below. There are two bays – one opening to the south-east, and the other to the south-west, and between is a narrow isthmus of land. This enlarges to a promontory running south, on which the early quarries are sited. Everywhere are signs of the workmen's tools in the marble which slopes to the sea. Here the ships were able to load unless the weather was particularly inclement.

The bay which faces south-east forms an almost perfect land-locked

The island of Kinyra

Inscription from sanctuary at Aliki

harbour, at the side of which – on the narrow isthmus – is a small sanctuary, which dates originally from the middle of the seventh century BC. This sanctuary was in use continuously from its building, until Christianity became general throughout the island. The remains of two buildings are here, which were built on identical plans. They were nearly square (11 m 60 × 13 m and 15 m × 16 m 50). The building to the south had a porch of five Doric columns between two pillars *in antis*, dating to approximately 500 BC, and is the oldest Doric construction in the island.

The northern building, which was of much the same design, but slightly more complex, is in a far worse state of decay.

Unhappily, the original excavation, if excavation it can be called, was carried out with little scientific knowledge or care, and, as in the Passage of the *theoroi* the result was destruction rather than excavation. In this case, sadly, the excavator was an Englishman. He discovered one Archaic *kouros* and shipped this to the museum in Istanbul.

Inscriptions were found on blocks from the fallen walls wishing a good voyage to the marble ships Herakles, Serapis, Poseidon, Artemis, and Asclepios.

Another inscription recorded thanks to the Dioscures, the Saviour or Deliverer gods, who were the traditional protectors of those who went down to the sea in ships.

So far no other dedication has been found in either sanctuary. However another well-cut inscription hopes for a fair voyage for Heracleites, Eutychetus, and Thessaloniketus.

The remains of a Byzantine basilica on the hill above the ancient quarries dates the ending of the use of the two sanctuaries below. Another church was also found, near the south-easterly bay, with the remains of a chancel, and some moulded marbles.

A short distance from the sanctuaries are two cult-grottos with fragments of a dedication to Apollo; and a short distance to the south-east another grotto contained a quantity of ex-votos, pottery, and figurines, mainly of the Archaic period.

It must be presumed that the original colonists, among whom are likely to have been skilled workers in marble when living in Paros,

Sanctuary at Aliki. Note the base of a Doric column in the top picture and the entrance to the cult-grotto behind in the lower picture

prospected the island from the sea. From a boat they could have seen the marble cliffs of this part of the coast glittering for a long distance. Here was an obvious place to start workings, in the island which they must have known – or at any rate hoped – had marble among its natural resources; and here also, ready-made, was not one, but two natural harbours.

There are traces of another building by the south-western bay, but as yet no work has been started there.

Thasos had its own coinage, examples of which can be seen in the museum. Coinage was started soon after the colonization, during the second half of the sixth century BC, and the excavators have produced detailed descriptions of these coins, grouped in dates from 525 BC, until the second half of the first century AD, in the Guide de Thasos (Boccard – 1968). Most of the coins were bronze or silver, but there was some gold, minted some time between 404 and 340 BC. There is a tiny gold drachma of the earliest period, showing the god Herakles as an archer. Also of this period is a silver coin which shows two realistic dolphins.

The well-known early Thracian satyr carrying off a maenad is depicted on a number of the earliest silver coins, and this is also shown on some early coins minted in bronze, as is Herakles. The Herakles figure continued to the first century BC, only the later coins show a standing, rather than a kneeling figure.

Not unnaturally the coinage of the fourth century BC appears to be better produced, and there are one or two silver pieces stamped with the Thasian wine-amphora.

Coins are a highly specialized subject, but there are certainly some Thasian examples to interest the expert.

Thasian wine was famous, and at times was produced in very considerable quantity. Thasian wine-seals, stamped on excavated amphora, have been found all round the eastern Mediterranean, and as far west as Sicily, and it is known that Thasian vinegar was used in Rome.

Impressed seal on wine amphora of fourth century

Much enlarged photograph of Thasian silver coin of approximately 465 BC, *showing the common Thracian theme of maenad and satyr*

The excellence of the island wine was praised in Athens as early as the fifth century BC, and Aristophanes' circle knew the delights of the 'little Thasian amphorae . . .'

Much, in fact, was written in its praise, and it is sad that this industry has virtually ceased to exist. Although modern bottles bear a copy of a comparatively ancient label the island today does not grow many grapes, and such wine as there is is made on the nearby mainland.

During the fourth century BC, however, Thasos wine ranked high throughout the Mediterranean, and must have considerably increased the wealth of the already wealthy island. Theophrastus states that the wine was of 'a marvellous flavour' and there are many other comments still extant praising its bouquet, and its general excellence.

The most ancient Greek law of the wine and vinegar trade was found in Thasos, in 'boustrophedon' writing, concerning wine consecrated to Athena Poliouchos, and to the Pythian Apollo. There was also a regulation of the fifth century BC, concerning the sale of wine in *pithoi*, and yet another law concerned the export of wine, and the special magistrates who were concerned with this. (*IG. XII. suppl. 347.*)

A *sekoma* engraved on a marble tablet was excavated from the agora, dedicated by an *agoranome* (market policeman) to the god Hermes. This can be seen in the local museum. Very large numbers of *amphorae* were made in the Thasian potteries, of local clay veined with mica, and although the greatest number of these have been excavated in the island, they have also been found in Egypt and Sicily, on the Adriatic and Ilyrian coasts, and as far afield as Kabul, and Susa. The engraved stamps were of various designs, and presumably belonged to the vineyard, or to the merchant shipping the wine. The first stamped *amphora* dated to the fifth century BC but the majority were of the fourth and third centuries BC.

In *The Journal of Hellenic Studies* (1909) John ff. Baker-Penoyre wrote, at the end of his publication of the work done by him on Thasos in 1907:

I cannot leave Thasos without considering for a moment its political situation, and its future. The Egyptian ascendancy is dead. Of the Turkish ad-

ministration of the island at the time of my visit (1907) the inhabitants had little cause to complain, but they are the heirs of its past unhappy history. For this melancholy record the Turk can hardly be blamed. They failed, as every power since antiquity has failed, to keep the island free from the curse of sea thieves attracted by the cover given by pathless forests reaching to the water's edge. From these aggressors the island was never really free until the time came when the Mediterranean was dotted with steamers which could outpace the best-handled caique. Centuries of apprehension and insecurity have left their mark on the inhabitants who are apathetic and despairing to a marked degree. The few simple industries have fallen into disuse. The great limekilns of a generation ago are already mouldering away. I have come across masses of mouldering beeskips, and have never seen or tasted honey in the island. [Today – 1976 – some thousands of tons are produced every year, much of which is exported. J. W-T.]
There is good potter's clay in the north, but the horrible empty petroleum tin from the Black sea has killed the potter's art. For the mining industry, carried on successfully in the south-west of the island they show little aptitude ... So beautiful and richly endowed a spot will not, under the new conditions, long escape notice. For better or for worse it will pass again into the political furnace. In good or evil days those who know Thasos must needs wish it well.

Today the island is a thriving, and mainly hard-working place, with an already large and growing tourist trade. Fast ferries from Keramoti, and from Kavala, carry not only cars and foot-passengers to and from the island, but also innumerable lorries and other forms of heavy transport, bringing all types of supplies, and taking away the not inconsiderable exports of today.

Glossary

(In order in text)

THEOROI – 'observers'. In Thasos eponymous magistrates

PHYLAKOI – guardians at gates of a city

POLIS – city state

METOCHI – farm

CHITON – tunic

HIMATION – outer garment

KANTHAROS – two-handled drinking vessel

THIASOS – group of persons connected with the worship of a god

IN ANTIS – Latin term designating traditional plan of the porch of a Greek temple

PATRAI – In Thasos certain civic groups or families

CELLA – principal room of a Greek temple, containing the cult-statue

PRONAOS – entrance to above

KOUROS – nude statue of a young man of the Archaic period

PEPLOS – 'Dorian' garment worn by women

PINAKES – large votive plates

CHIMERA – mythological beast

ARYBALLOI – small scent bottles

POLOI – high cylindrical head-dresses

KORE – draped female statue

LEKANIS – plate or dish with lid

HIEROMEMON – In Thasos a deputy concerned with religious finance

BACCHAE – Female followers of Dionysos. Play by Euripides

THYRSOS – giant fennel stem decorated with ivy

DITHYRAMB – choral song to Dionysos – cult song

CHOES – small jug used for ritual drinking

PANSPERMIA – a mixture of fruits and seeds cooked on the third day of the festival Anthesteria

PARADOI – entrance passages on either side of a Greek stage

KERYKEION – herald's staff
APOLOGOI – In Thasos magistrates for justice
PITHOI – large storage jars for wine
SEKOMA – table of wine measurements engraved on marble
AGORANOME – market policeman
AMPHORA – wine jar

Archaic Period	720–480 BC
Classical Period	480–323 BC
Hellenistic Period	323–27 BC

Bibliography

Herodotus. *The Histories*

Thucydides. *The Pelopponesian War*

Pausanias. *Guide to Greece*

Hippocrates. 'Epidemics'

J. M. Edmonds (translation). *Elegy and Iambus*

Charbonneaux–Villard–Martin. *Archaic Greek Art*

— *Classical Greek Art*

Albin Lesky. *Greek Tragedy*

Euripides. *The Bacchae*. Translation Moses Hadas, and Greene,
     Latimore and Arrowsmith.

G. S. Kirk. *Greek Myths*

Martin Nilsson. *Cults, Myths etc. in Ancient Greece*

N. G. L. Hammond. *A History of Greece to 322 B.C*

A. R. Burn. *A History of Greece*

Arnold J. Tonybee. *Greek Historical Thought*

John Boardman. *Pre-Classical – From Crete to Archaic Greece*

Guy Pentreath. *Hellenic Traveller*

R. P. Winnington-Ingram. *Euripides and Dionysos*

C. Roebuck. *Ionian Trade and Colonisation*

École Française d'Athenes. *Guide de Thasos* (1968)

Charles Picard. *Monuments et Memoires* (Eugene Piot)

American Journal of Archaeology. Pouilloux (1959)

— Salviat (1960)

Bulletin de Correspondance Hellénique. (BCH) E. Miller,
     J. Pouilloux, R. Martin, Fr. Salviat, N. Weill

Journal of Hellenic Studies (JHS) J. ff. Baker Penoyre,
     Th. Bent, Haspels

Etudes Thasiennes (ET)

Inscriptions Graecae. (IG) Thasos